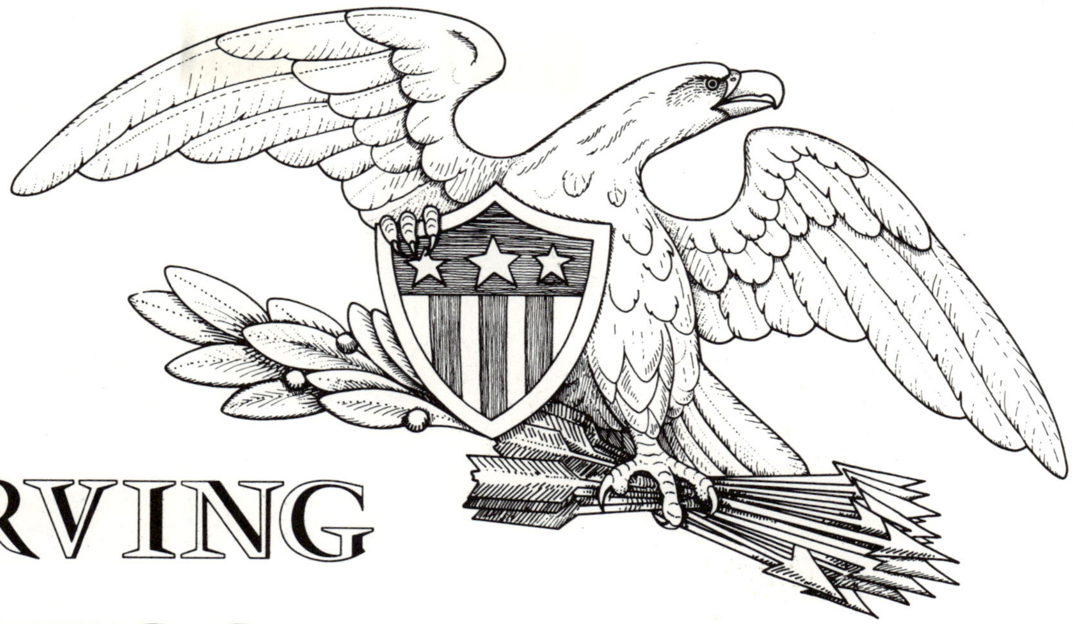

CARVING DECORATIVE EAGLES

FULL-SIZE PATTERNS FOR 10 PROJECTS

by

Anthony Hillman

Dover Publications, Inc., New York

Published in Canada by General Publishing Company, Ltd., 30 Lesmill Road, Don Mills, Toronto, Ontario.
Published in the United Kingdom by Constable and Company, Ltd.

Carving Decorative Eagles: Full-Size Patterns for 10 Projects is a new work, first published by Dover Publications, Inc., in 1989.

Manufactured in the United States of America
Dover Publications, Inc., 31 East 2nd Street, Mineola, N.Y. 11501

Library of Congress Cataloging-in-Publication Data

Hillman, Anthony.
Carving decorative eagles : full-size patterns for 10 projects / by Anthony Hillman.
p. cm.
ISBN 0-486-25976-5
1. Wood-carving—Patterns. 2. Eagles in art. I. Title.
TT199.7.H536 1989
736′.4—dc19 89-1533
CIP

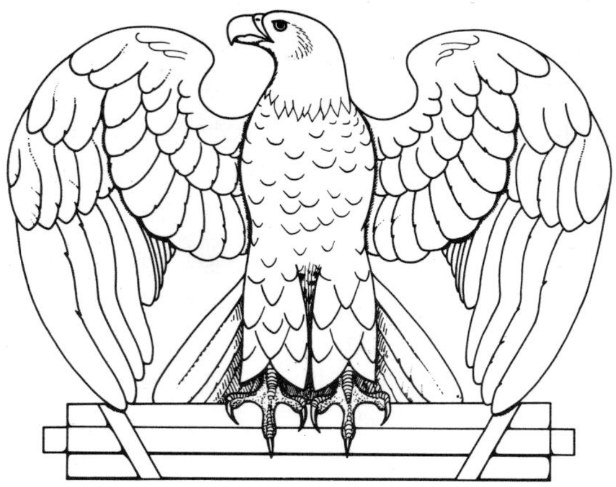

How to Carve Decorative Eagles

Eagles have long been regarded as symbols of freedom and power. The Bald (or American) Eagle (*Haliaeetus leucocephalus*), being the only eagle both native to North America and found nowhere else, was appropriately adopted as an official national emblem by an act of Congress on June 20, 1782. From that time, an image of the Bald Eagle was prominently displayed on the seal of the United States of America, to this day printed on every dollar bill. A natural consequence of the government's symbolic adoption of this powerful bird of prey was its appearance as the central element of countless patriotic decorations of all different kinds and varying degrees of artistic sophistication. Soon majestic images of Bald Eagles, frequently clutching banners, shields, and arrows, graced buildings, ships, and mantels throughout the United States.

The ten decorative carvings in this book are modeled after traditional nineteenth- and early twentieth-century carvings of Bald Eagles. Two projects are carvings "in the round"; the others are relief carvings. The bas-relief bookends (Plate 11), while incorporating traditional elements, are of my own design. The first seven projects were designed with flat backs and are especially suitable for use as plaques, ideal for displaying on mantels, walls, flat sterns of boats, and so on.

Many of the originals after which these carvings were modeled, particularly those showing eagles with wings fully spread, were executed on a large scale and measured several feet across. The patterns here are limited to about 17" across, but they may be enlarged (or reduced) if you wish. There are many ways of doing this. The grid method, using graph paper, is one of the best and easiest. If you are unfamiliar with this method, you may wish to use *The Artist's and Craftsman's Guide to Reducing, Enlarging and Transferring Designs* by Rita Weiss (Dover 24142-4), which comes with a supply of special graph paper. If you use the patterns as exact-size templates, your carvings will be of a size suitable for attractive decorations over doorways, archways, or similar locations. Several of the templates may be used as patterns for sewing and other needlework projects. Those patterns that include banners allow for the application of lettering of your choice to convey patriotic, holiday, or personal messages.

To use the patterns, remove the staples from the book and spread the pages flat. Be sure to notice which patterns may be used as templates, and which are for reference only. You can cut out the templates and use them directly, but I recommend that you give them permanence by gluing them to 3/16" exterior plywood of high quality. Carefully recut the patterns and seal the edges with varnish. Preserved this way, these templates should last a lifetime.

When you have selected your project and determined its size, you should choose your wood (dimensions given on the plates apply to the size of the patterns used without reducing or enlarging). It is necessary to select good material to make a good carving. Suitable wood for these projects includes white pine, basswood, and mahogany (a favorite with colonial craftsmen). As you gain experience, you may want to try some harder woods, such as cherry, black walnut, or butternut. Be sure the wood is well seasoned. I prefer air-dried woods when available, but regular kiln-dried stock from lumberyards is usually suitable.

Always pay attention to the direction of the grain in the pieces of wood you select. On each pattern I have indicated the direction in which the grain should run in the finished carving. This is especially important in carving eagles with wings fully extended. Too much deviation from the proper grain direction will cause the slightest pressure applied in carving to result in damage to the wingtips, bill, or other fragile areas. The tip of the bill is the most vulnerable part, and I advise you to be especially careful when sawing out the bill patterns. Fine points and thin edges are most liable to inadvertent damage as you hold and brace the carving. Therefore you should leave as much wood as possible around all of the above-mentioned areas during the initial and middle stages of your work.

To carve these projects at the scale of the patterns, you will need a few standard wood-working tools, plus a very few additional tools especially suitable for relief carving. A band saw is the most practical tool for cutting out the patterns. If the project is not too big, however, a jigsaw or coping saw is fine. (I use a ¼″ blade in my band saw, but, if you intend to cut many fragile feather tips, a ⅛″ blade or a jigsaw would be better.) For general woodcarving purposes you will need several sharp knives. Remember, the broader the blade, the bigger the cutting radius. For relief carving you will need a few chisels as well as a few gouges of various sweeps. To make the carvings shown on the covers of this book, I used gouges with blades of ¼″ to 1″ wide. A gouge of ¼″ or ⅜″ with a sweep of #2 or #3 and two or three 1″ gouges with sweeps ranging from #3 to #8 will suffice. (The higher the number, the deeper the sweep, or curve of the blade as seen head-on.) For smoothing surfaces, you will need a small spokeshave, as well as sufficient cloth-backed sandpaper, with the fineness of the grit ranging from #60 through #80 to #100 or finer.

You may also find it convenient to use a wood-burning tool (pyroelectric pen) to burn some surface decoration onto softer woods. While not traditional, this can be a very effective and time-saving procedure if carefully done.

Carving an Eagle Plaque

Let's begin with the sternboard decoration on Plate 1. First study the pattern and the color photograph on the cover of this book showing the finished carving. Cut out the very rough outer form of the template on your piece of wood, remembering always the proper direction of the grain (do not yet cut into the area between the wings and the flag). This will give you what is known as a carving "blank." If you are unfamiliar with relief carving, it is especially important to take note of the following procedures. Before you make a single cut, obtain a clear idea of the relative depth of the various parts of your project. Generally, on the eagle plaques in this book, the heads, shields, arrows, banners, and feet are in the foreground, while the wings, tail, and middle body are in the background. Study the lines on the patterns, which are drawn so as to make clear the contours and divisions of the carving. Always keep a picture in your mind of the overall result you are aiming for as you carve each particular area. This way you will avoid irreparable mistakes, and, with a little care and common sense, you can make even a ¾″-thick plaque appear to possess much greater depth.

Now, using an ordinary lead pencil, trace the main outlines onto the wood. At this point do not mark any lines except the outlines of the wings, head, bill, legs, and feet, and then the flag (on other plaques, the shield, arrows, etc.). Do not mark or cut any feathers yet! At this time you should just contour-carve the general shape of the wings, referring to Figure 1, which shows an eagle wing in cross section. Since the back of the plaque, and therefore the wings, should be flat, work toward the cross-sectional shape shown in Fig. 2. Use a shallow-sweep gouge to scoop out

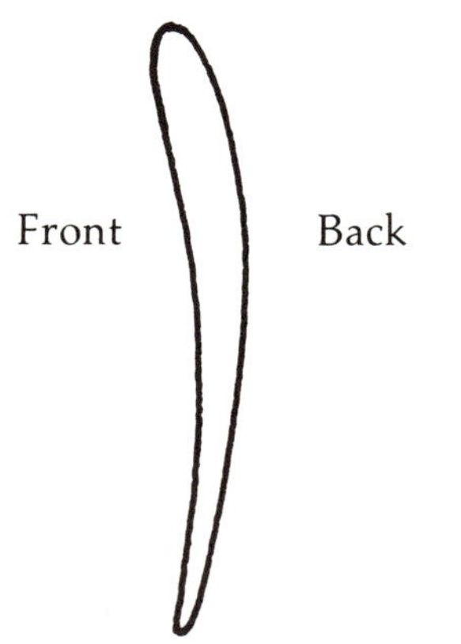

Fig. 1

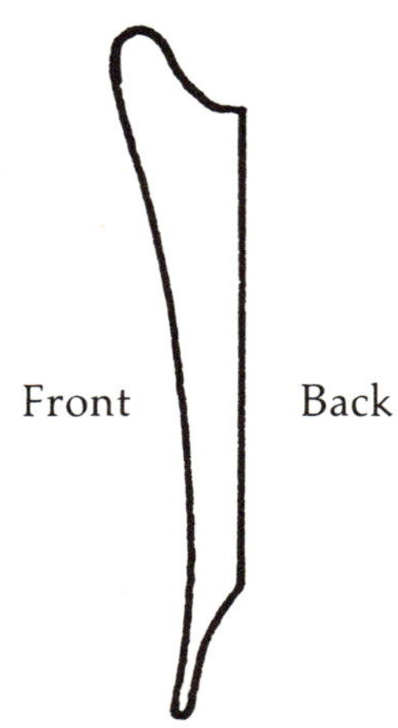

Fig. 2

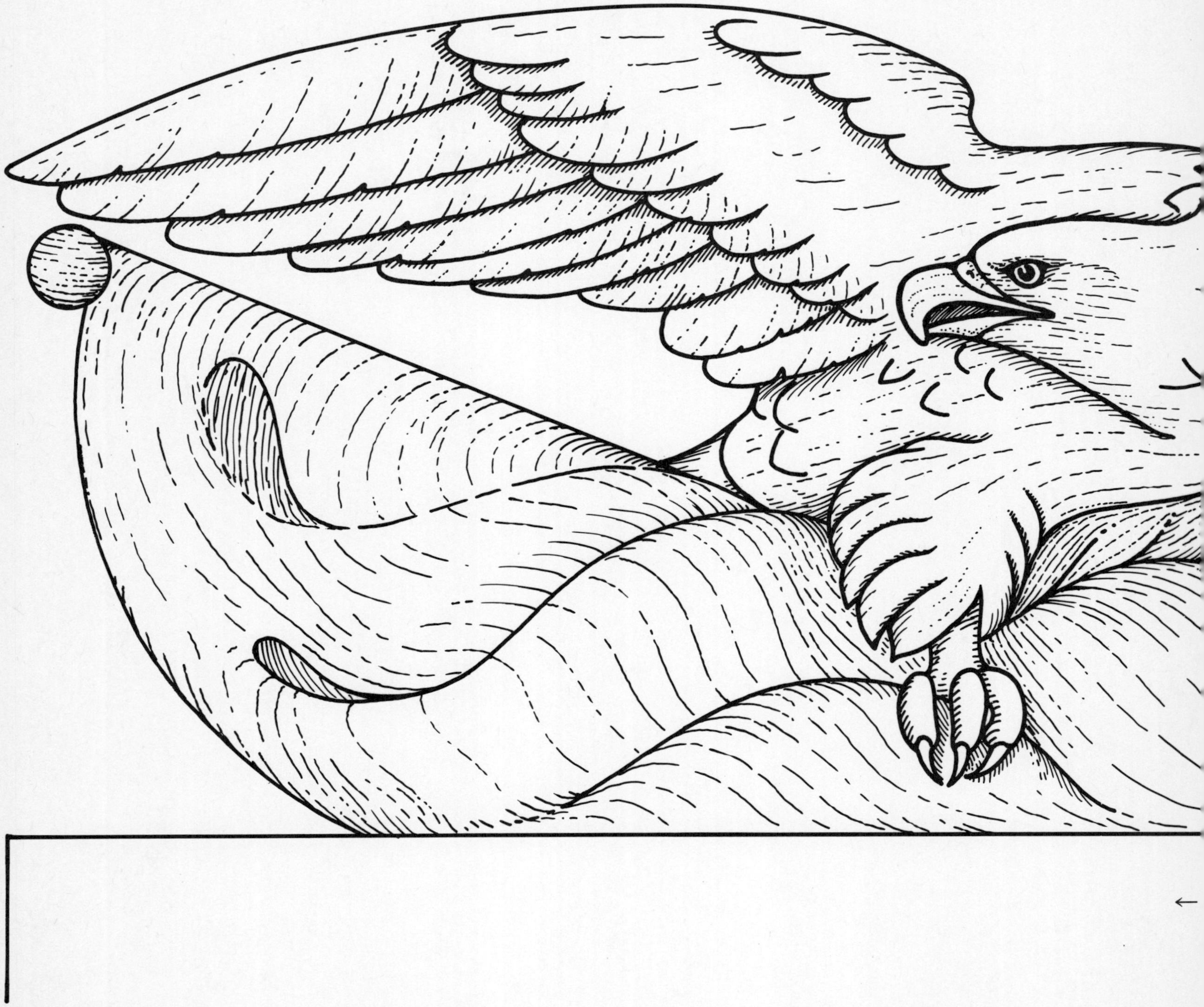

Sternboard Decoration

(late nineteenth-century design)

Wood: 2″ thick

Plate 1 (left) Remove staples to see and use full patterns.

Mantel Decoration

(based on carving by Samuel McIntire, 1806)

Wood: 2″ thick

Plate 2 (left) Remove staples to see and use full patterns.

Post Office Eagle

(based on ornament by Lombard & Ludwig
for Elgin, Texas, post office, 1938)

Wood: 2″ thick

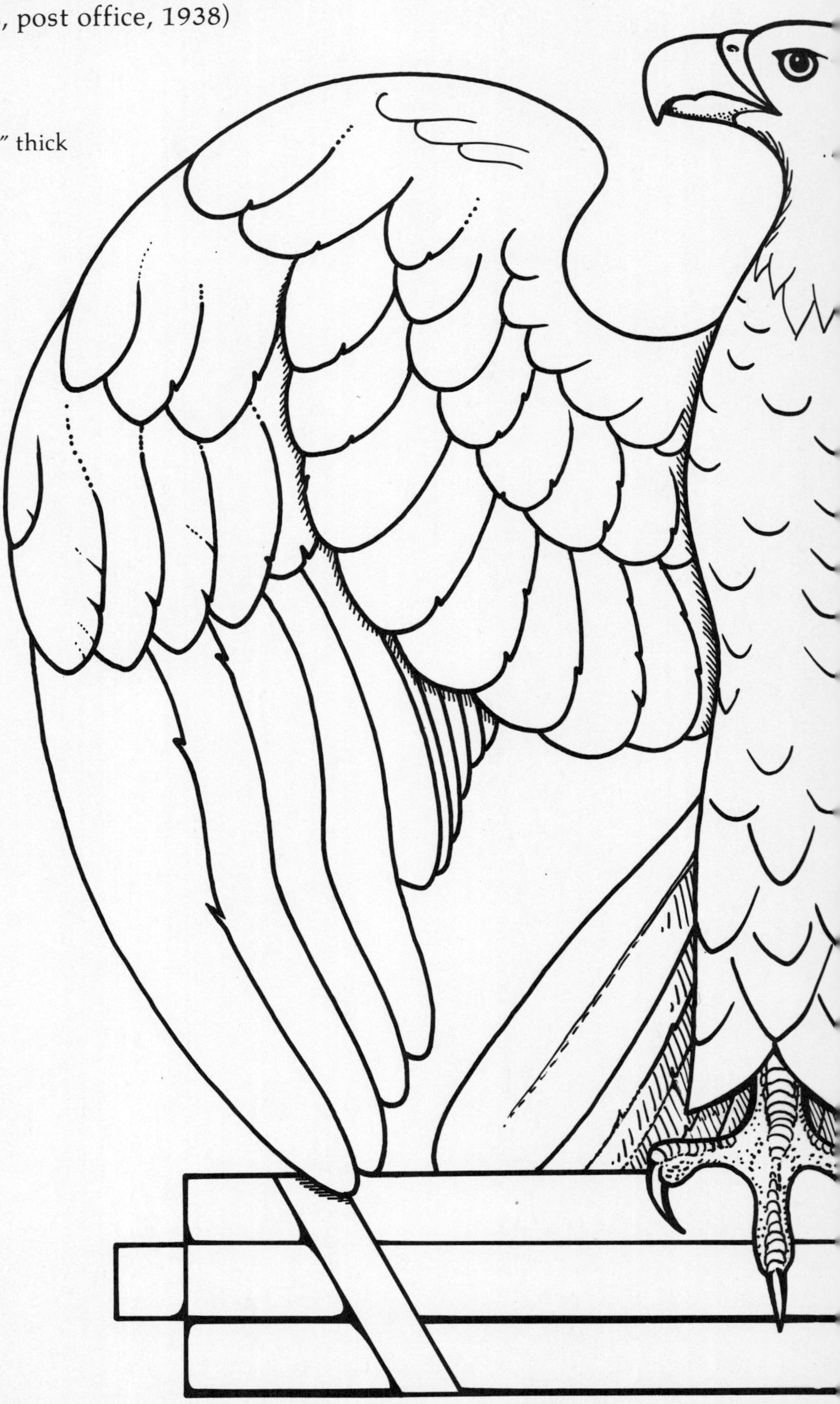

Plate 3 (left) Remove staples to see and use full patterns.

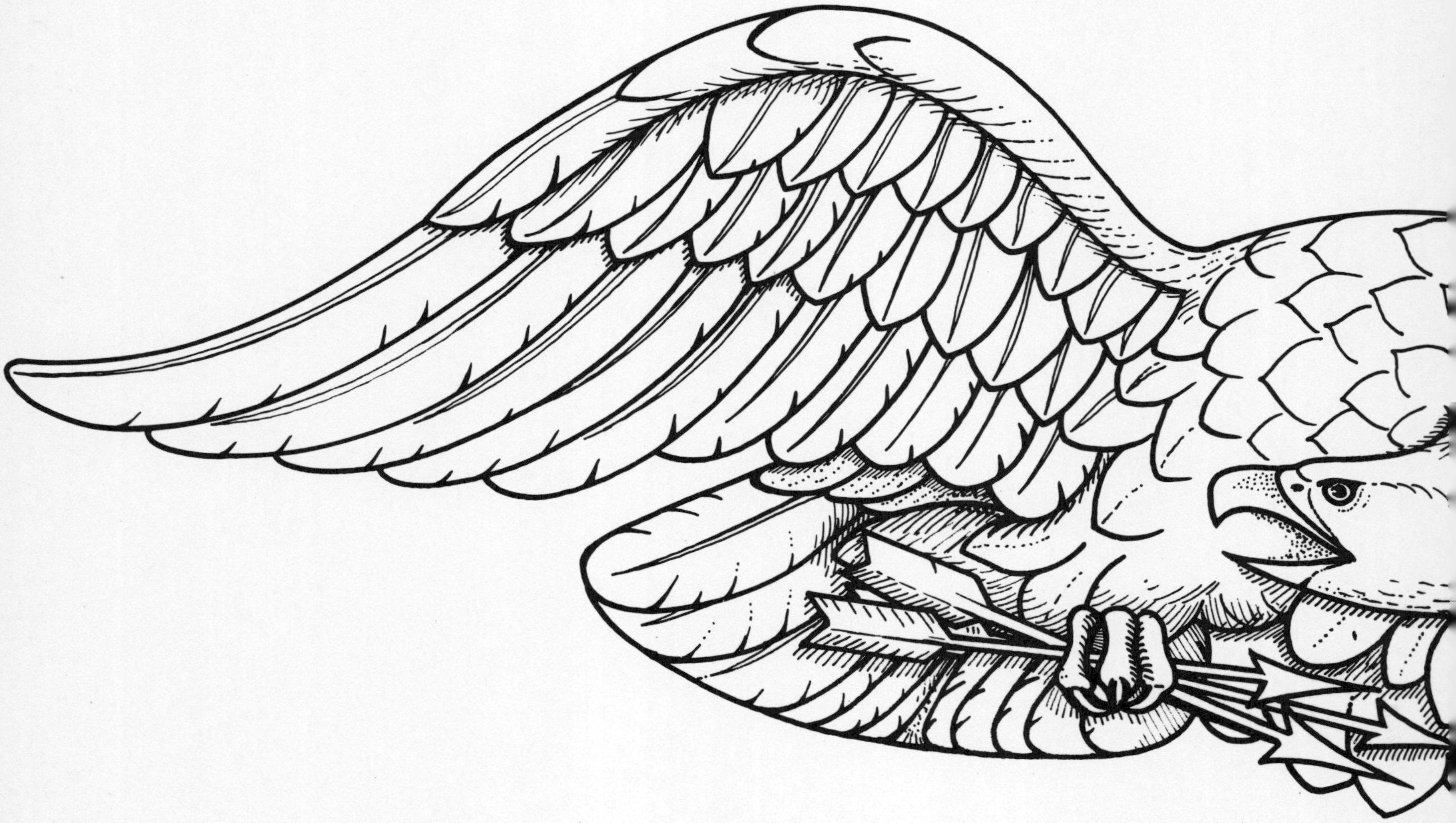

Eagle with Arrows and Shield

(nineteenth-century design)

Wood: 1½″ thick

Plate 4 (left) Remove staples to see and use full patterns.

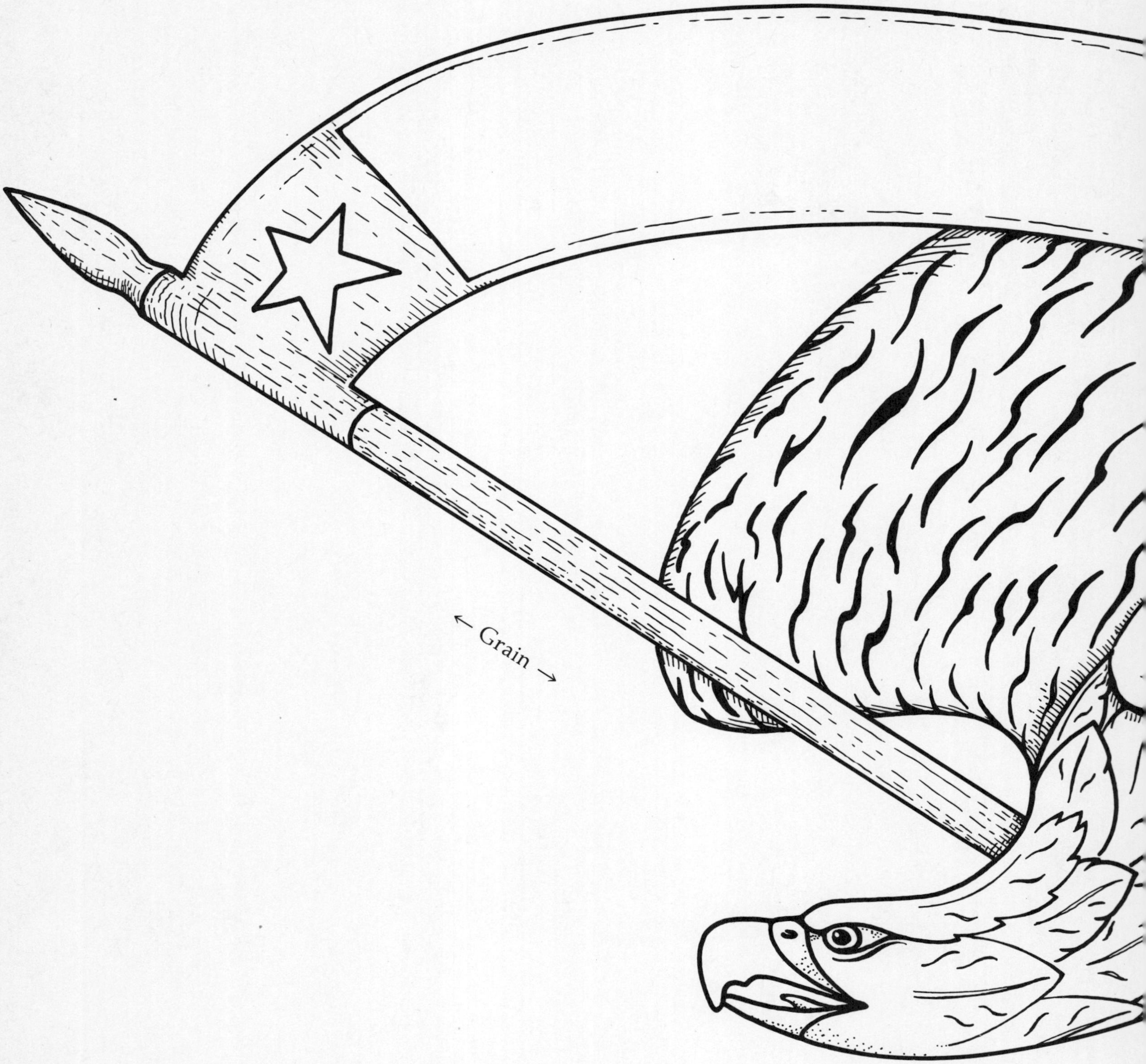

Eagle with Banner

(based on ship carving by John H. Bellamy
[1836–1914], Kittery, Maine)

Wood: 1½″ to 2½″ thick

Plate 5 (left) Remove staples to see and use full patterns.

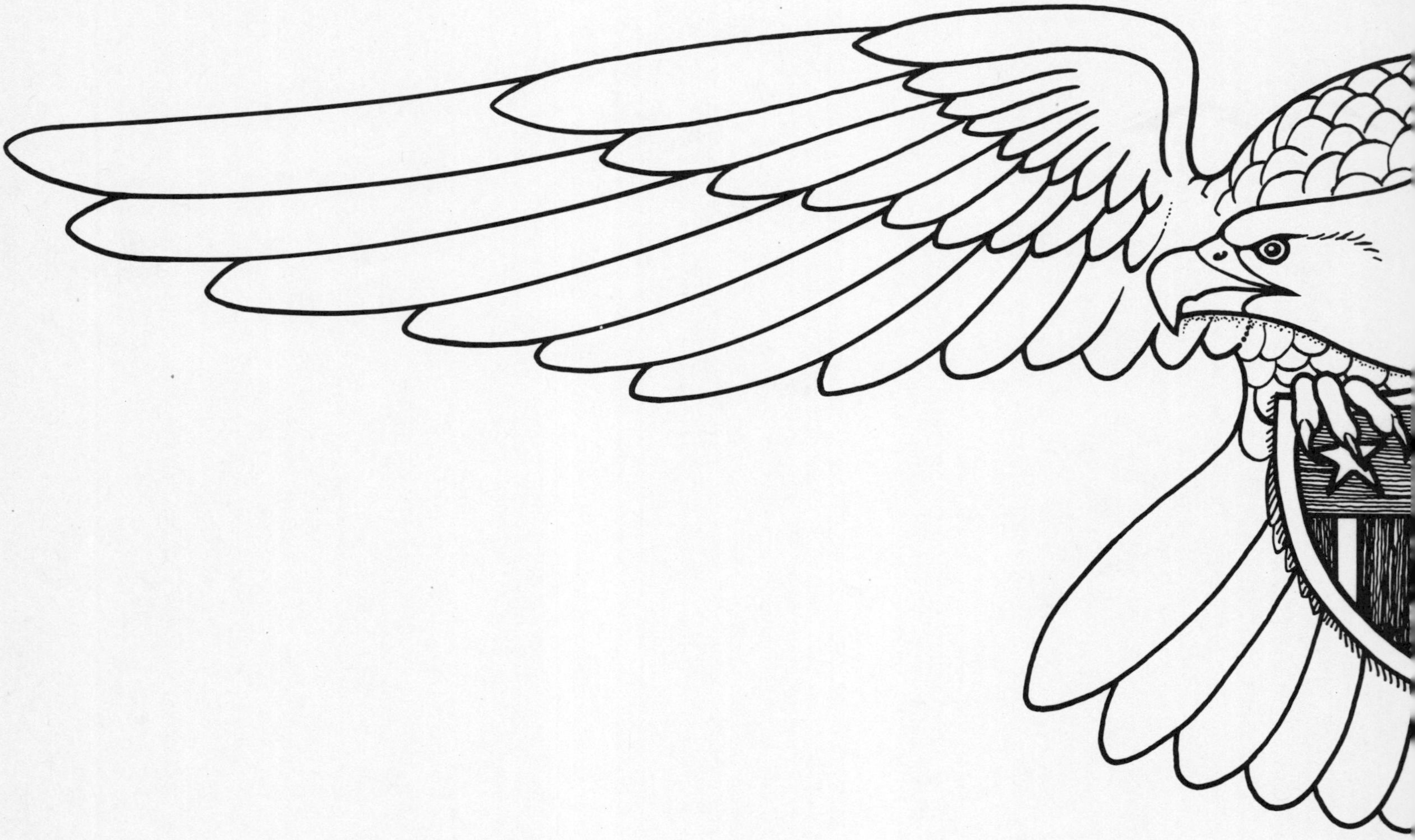

Sternboard Decoration

(nineteenth-century design)

Wood: 1″ thick

Plate 6 (left) Remove staples to see and use full patterns.

Eagle with Banner in Talons

(nineteenth-century design)

Wood: ¾″ to 2″ thick

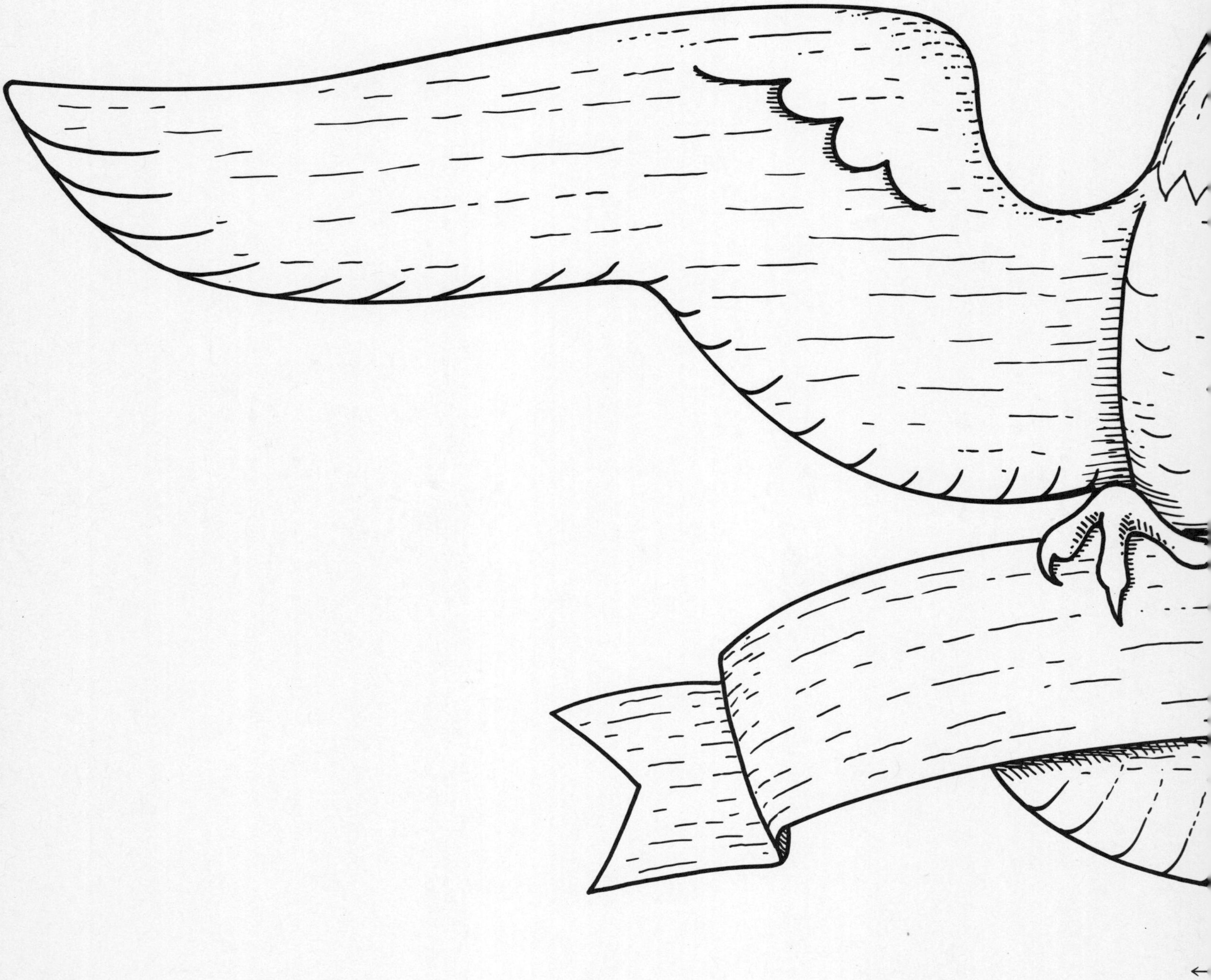

Plate 7 (left) Remove staples to see and use full patterns.

Standing Eagle—Body

(carved in the round)

Wood—Body and Base (including head and tail):
20″ long × 8″ wide × 8″ thick
Wings (two pieces): 14½″ long × 9″ wide × 1″ thick

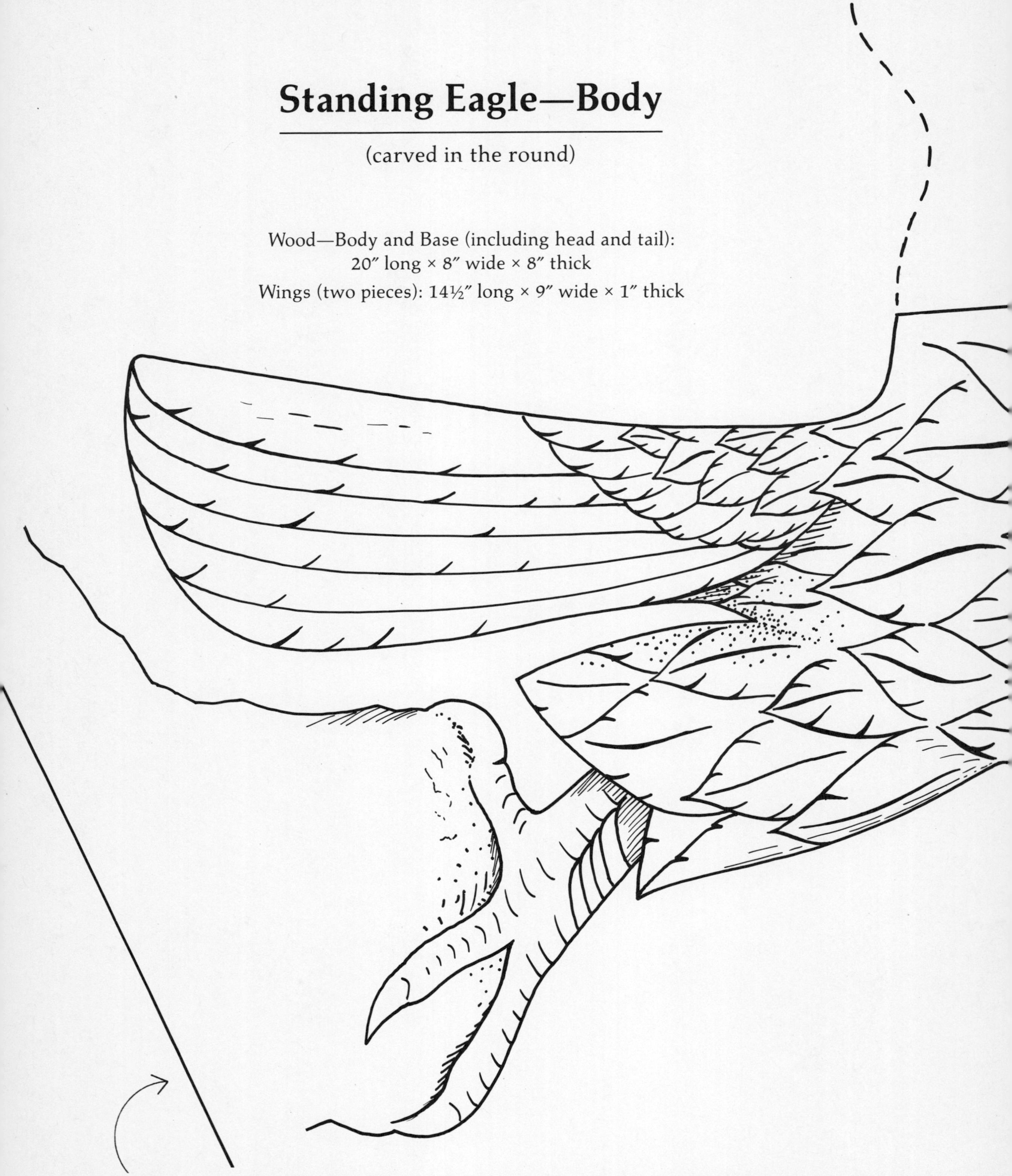

This line shows approximate angle of base. For best results, should actually be 3″ to 6″ from foot.

 Remove staples to see and use full patterns.

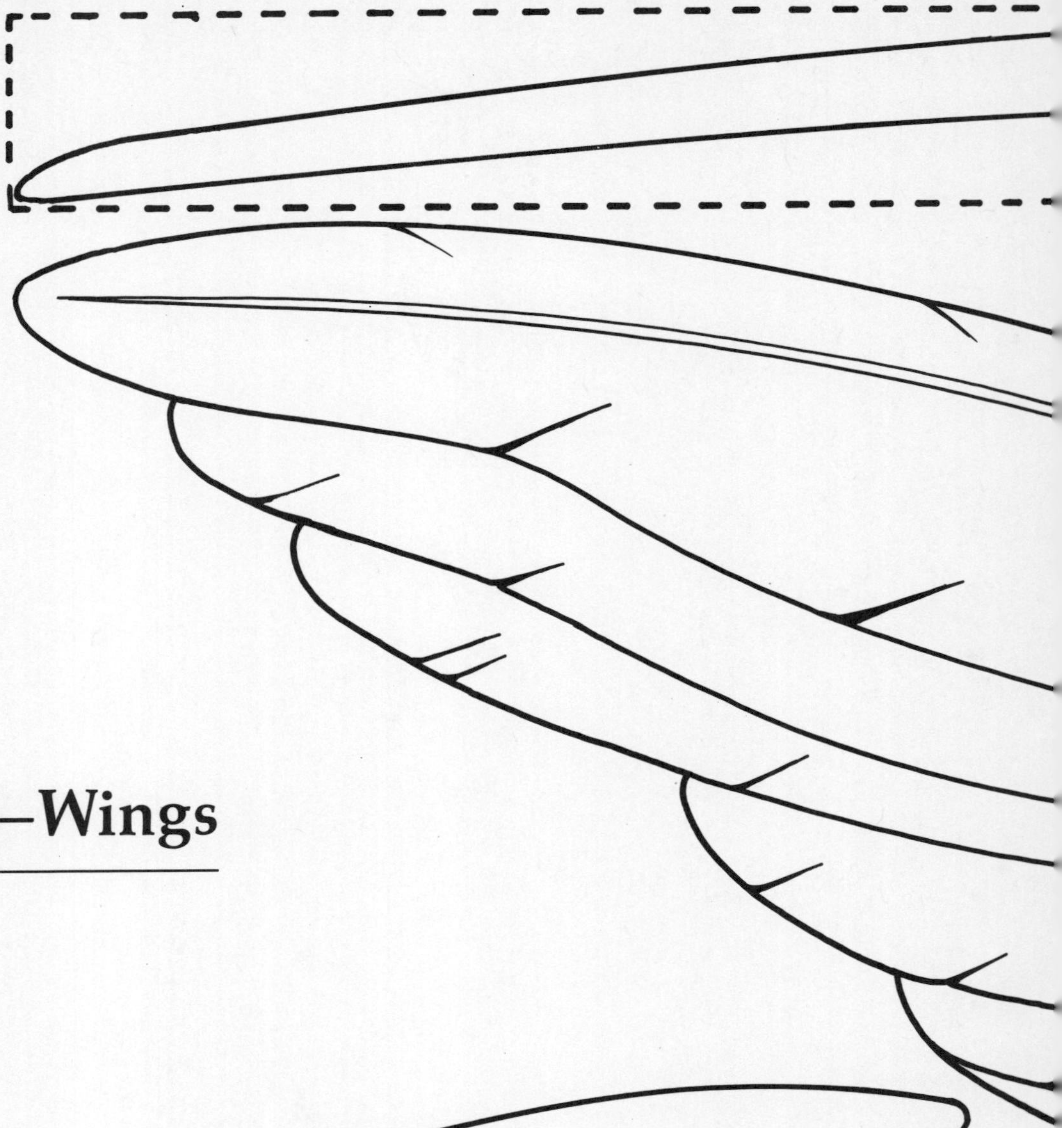

Standing Eagle—Wings

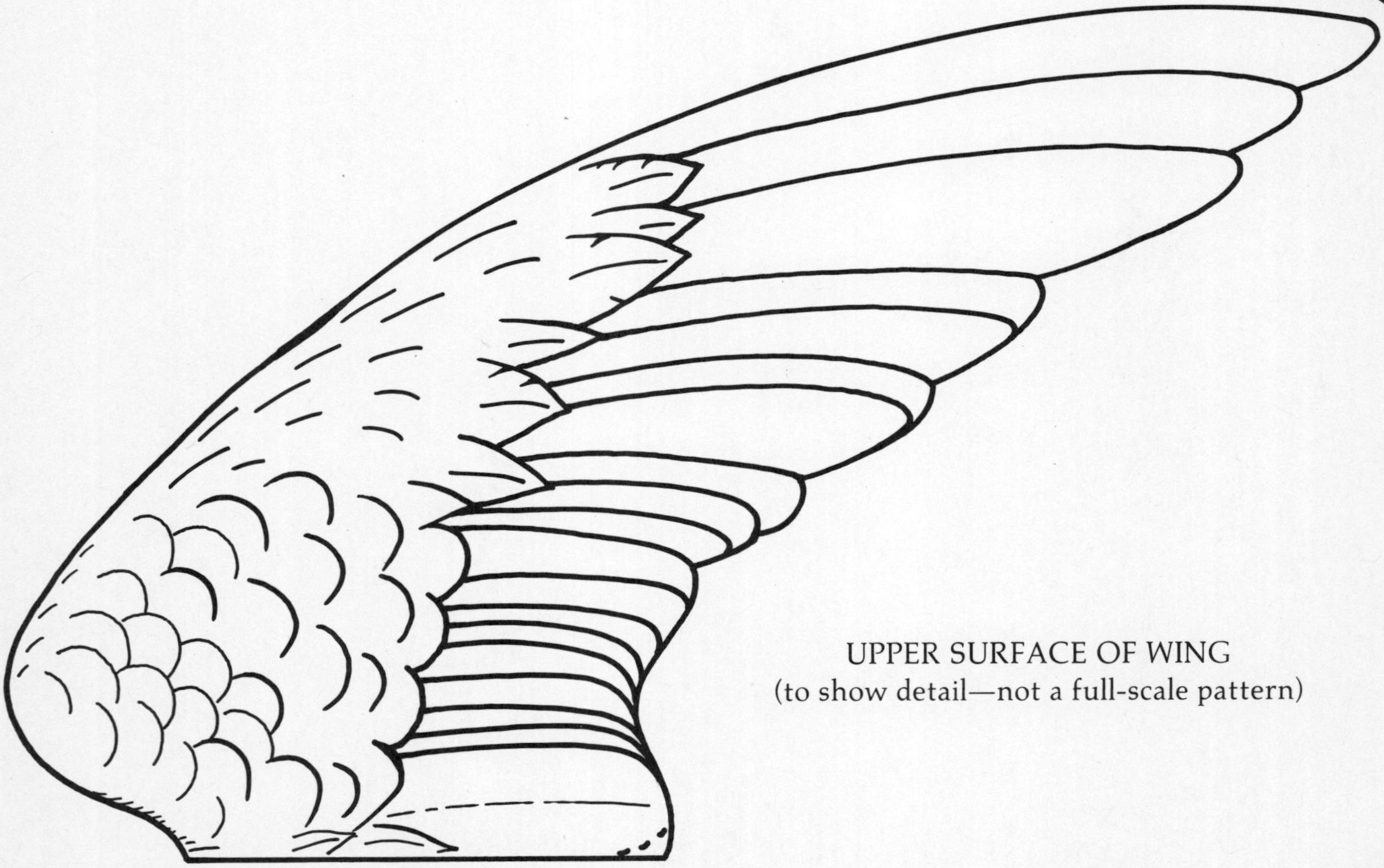

UPPER SURFACE OF WING
(to show detail—not a full-scale pattern)

Plate 9 (left) Remove staples to see and use full patterns.

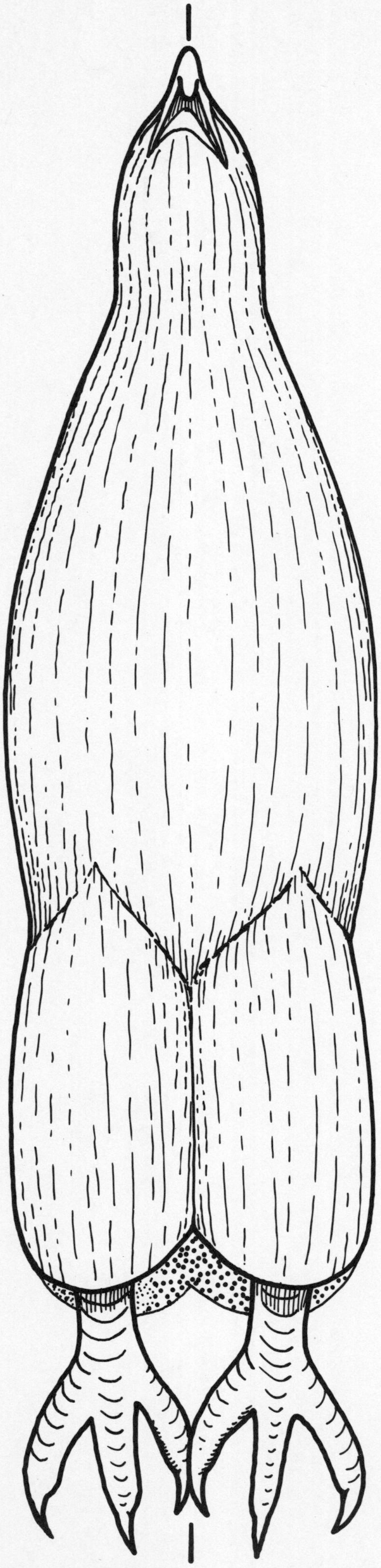

FRONT VIEW

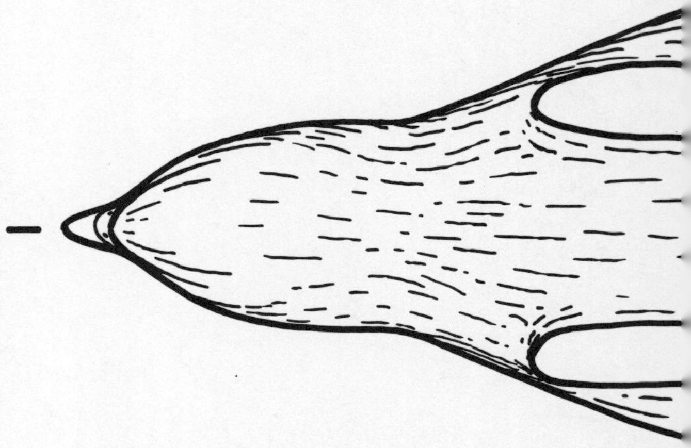

Plate 10 (left) Remove staples to see and use full patterns.

Bas-Relief Eagle Bookends

Wood (two pieces): 6″ long × 4¼″ wide × ¾″ thick

FRONT VIEW

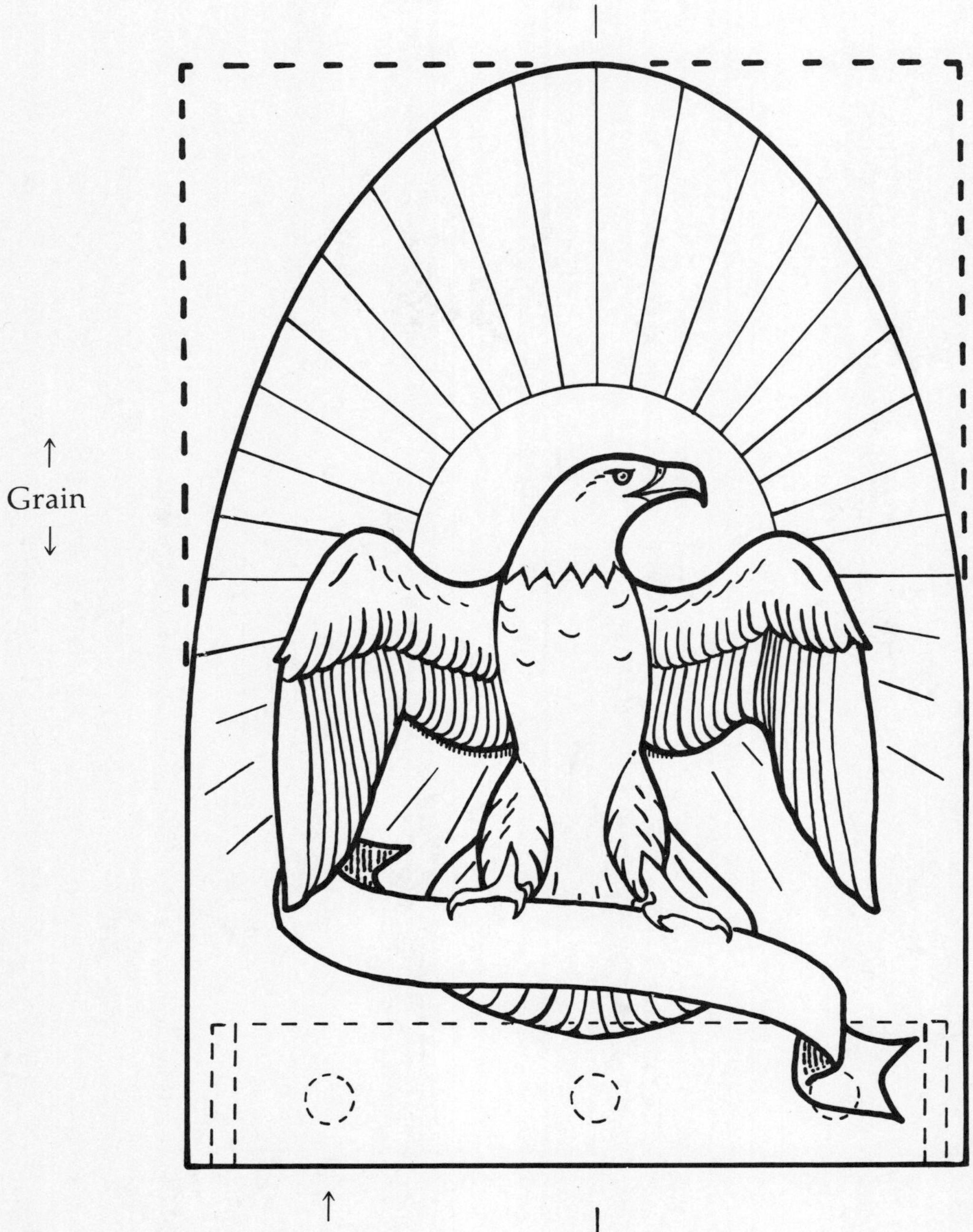

Plate 11 (left) Remove staples to see and use full patterns.

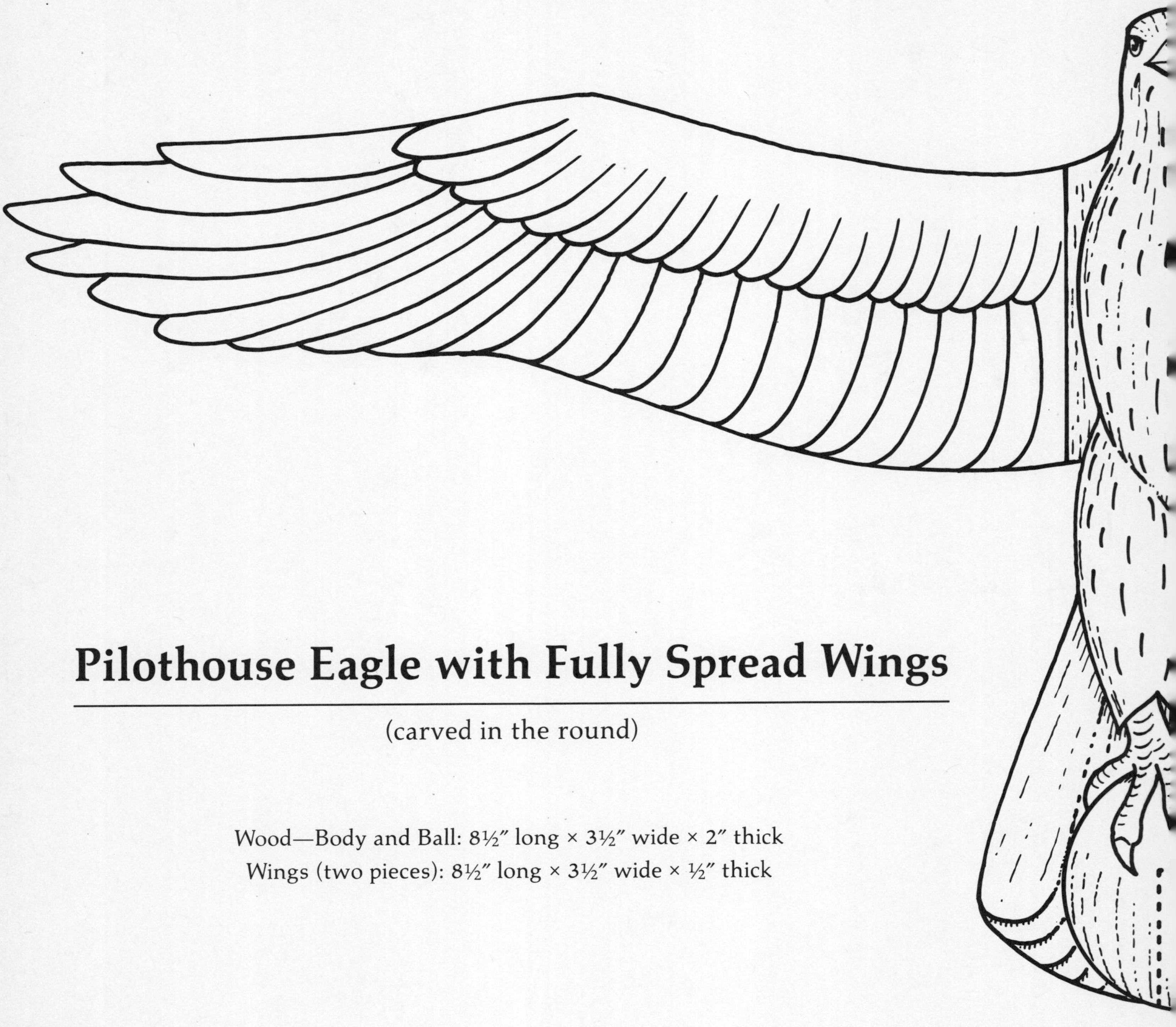

Pilothouse Eagle with Fully Spread Wings

(carved in the round)

Wood—Body and Ball: 8½″ long × 3½″ wide × 2″ thick
Wings (two pieces): 8½″ long × 3½″ wide × ½″ thick

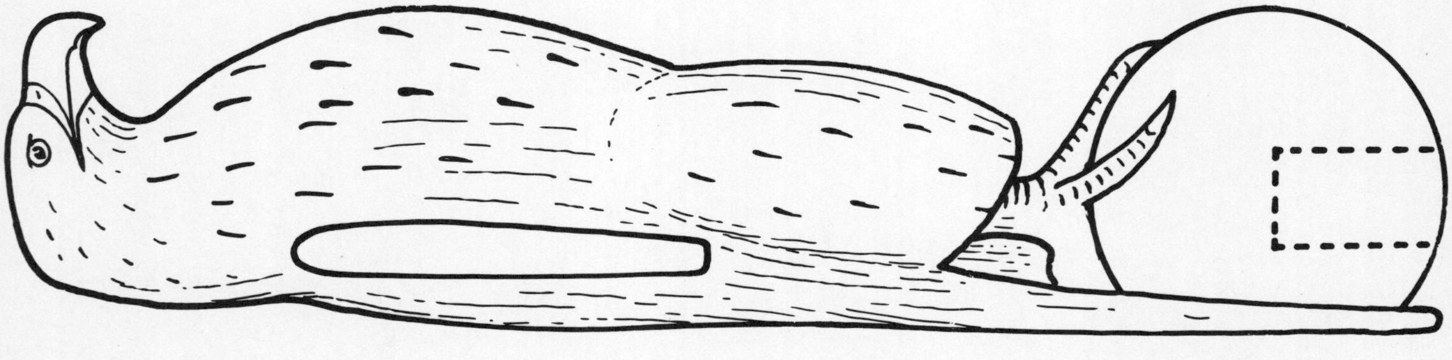

Drill

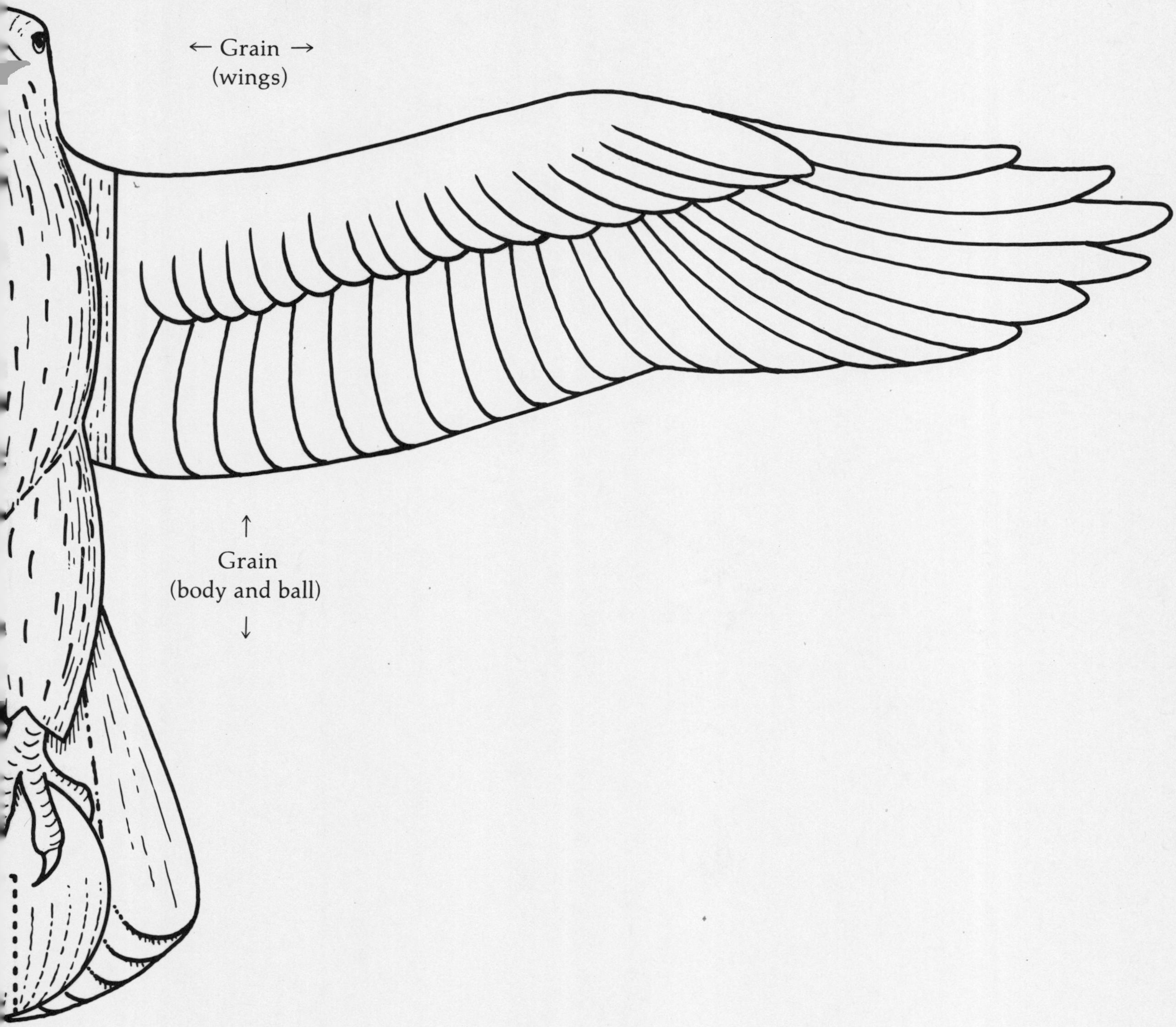

hole

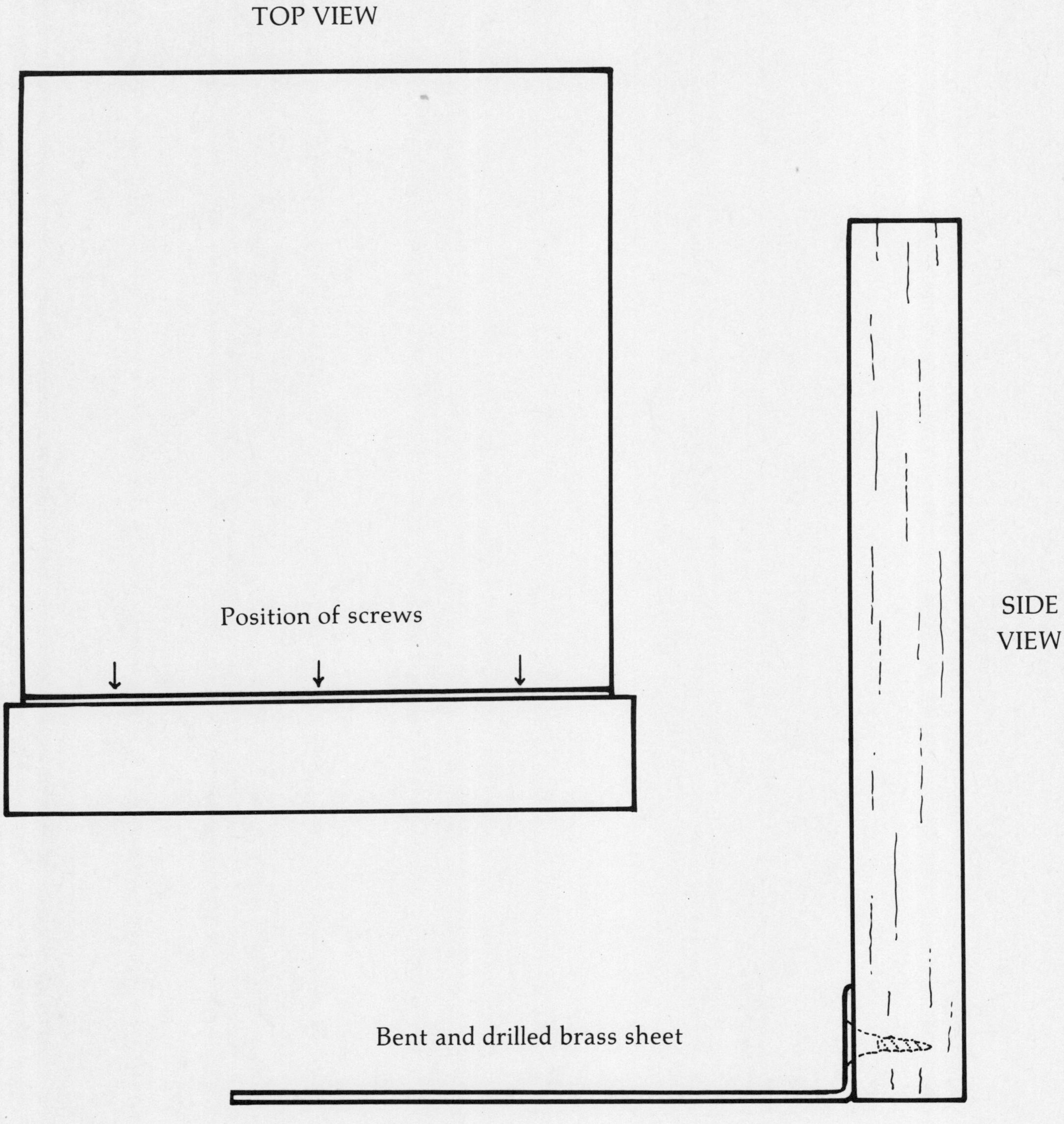

Metal for Base: brass sheet 1/16″ (.0625″) thick, 4″ × 10″, cut in half

Standing Eagle—Front and Rear Views

NOTE: These patterns are for reference only.

They are not full-size and cannot be used as templates.

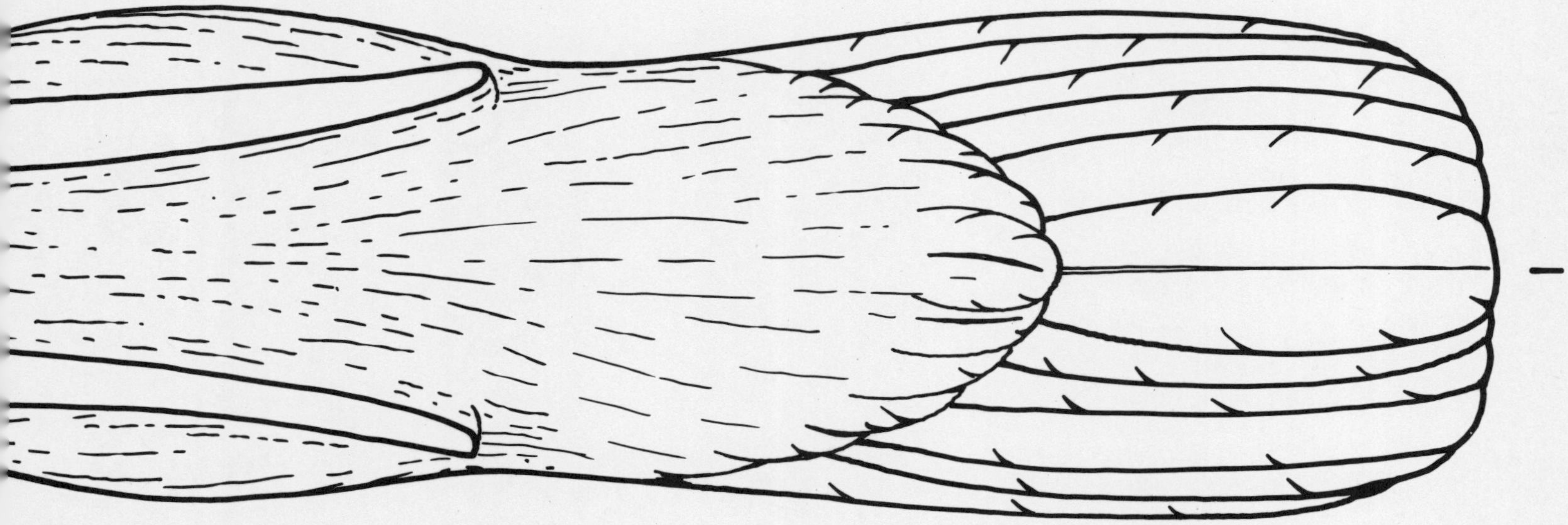

REAR VIEW

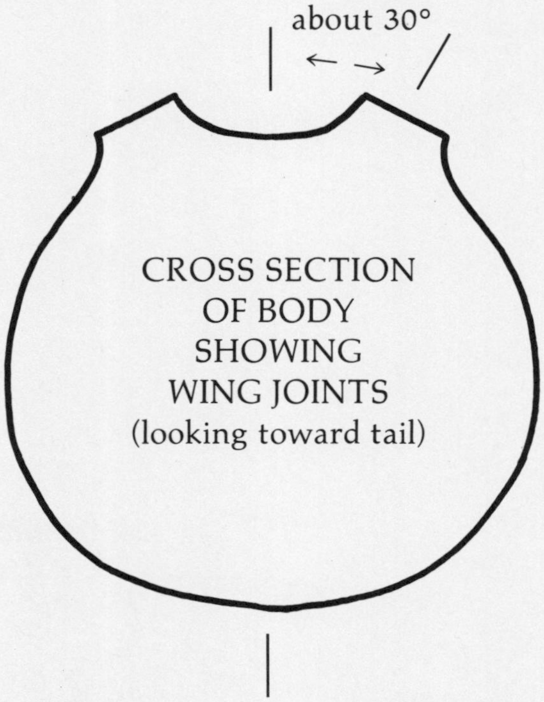

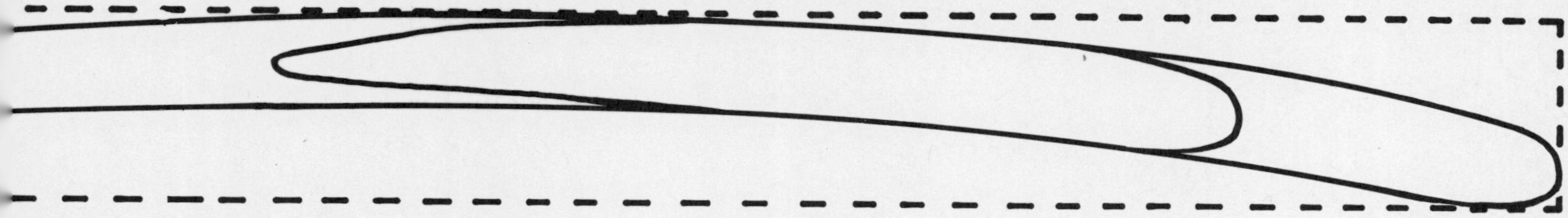

Cross section of wing, looking from base

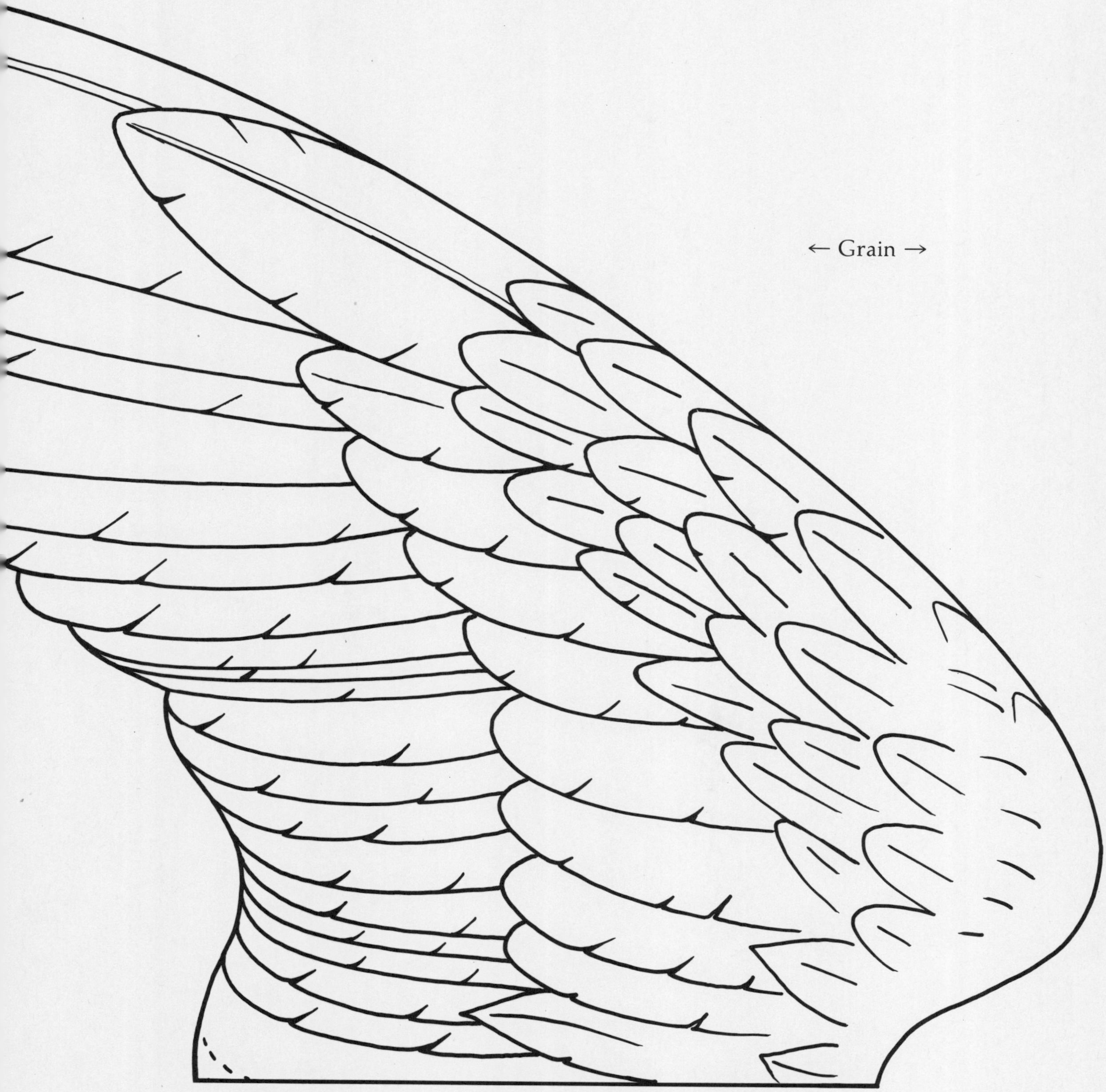

WING TEMPLATE (showing undersurface)
(flip shape over for other wing)

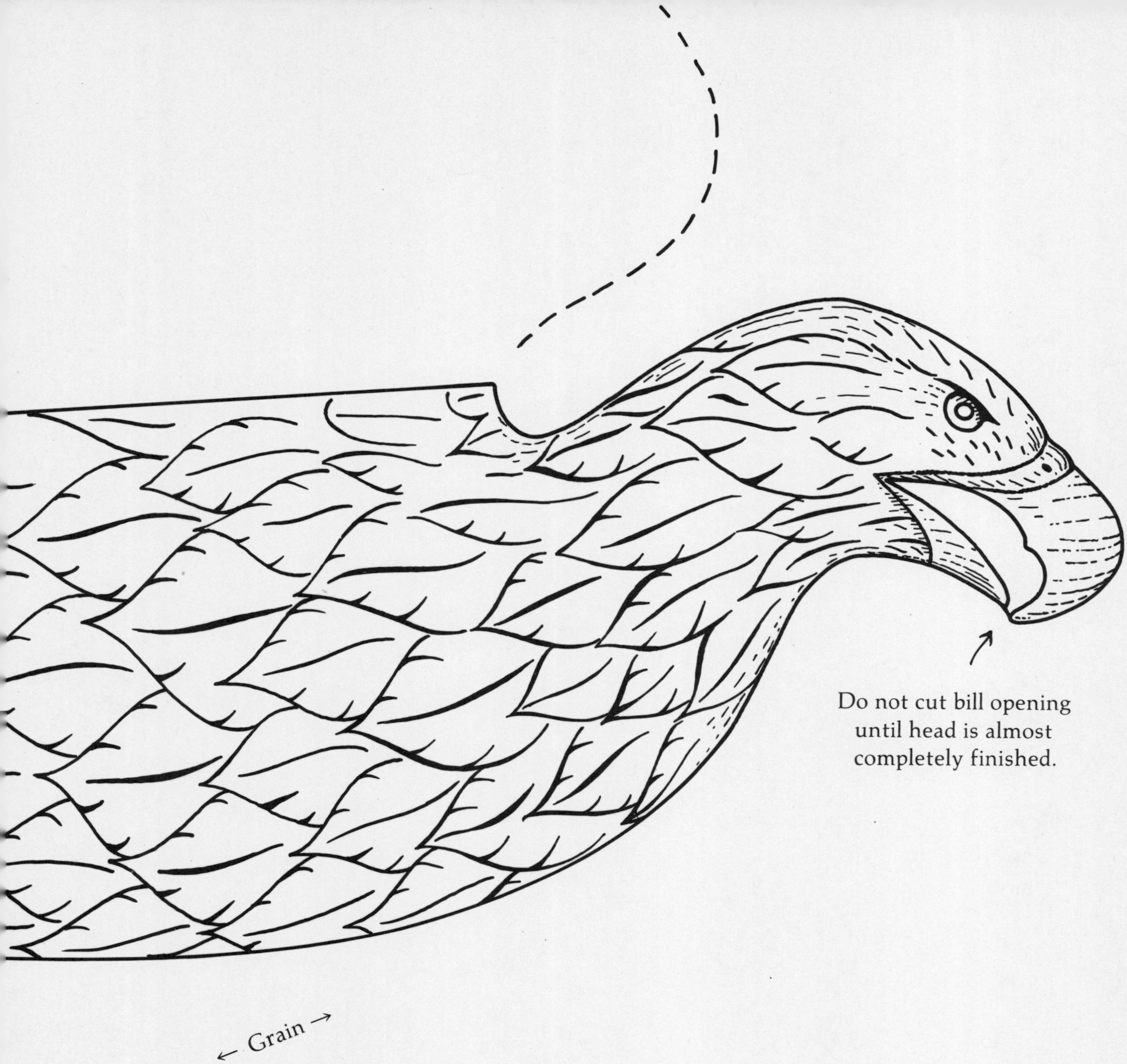

Do not cut bill opening until head is almost completely finished.
← Grain →

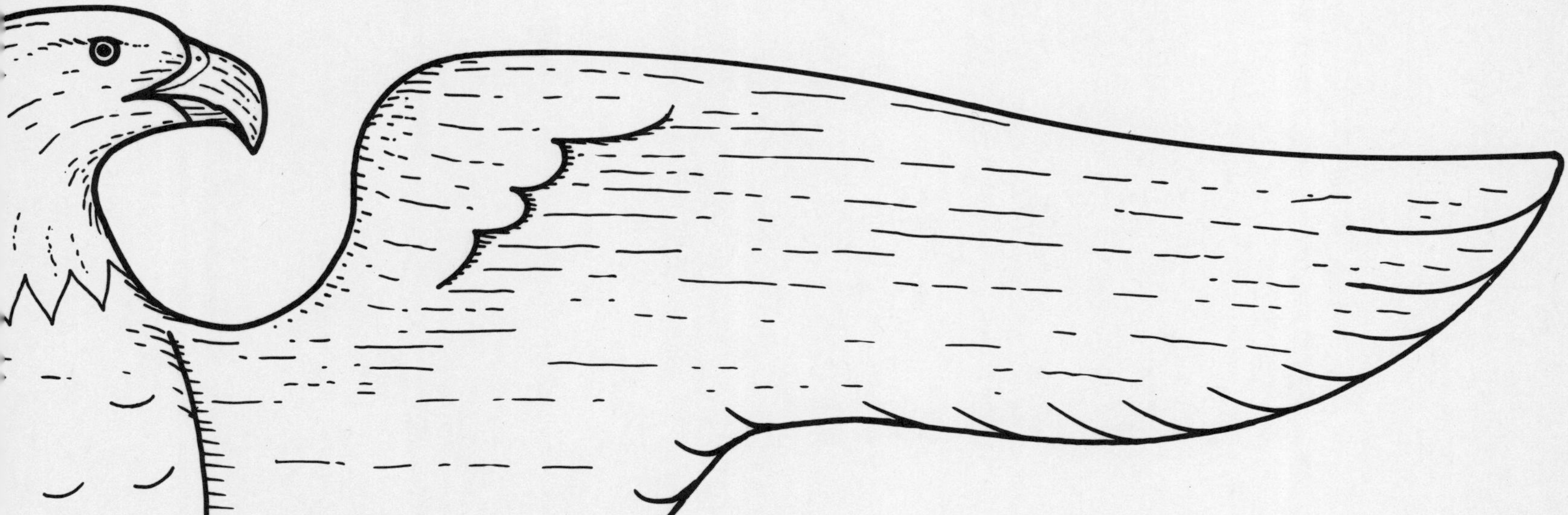

n →

Remove staples to see and use full patterns. ***Plate 7 (right)***

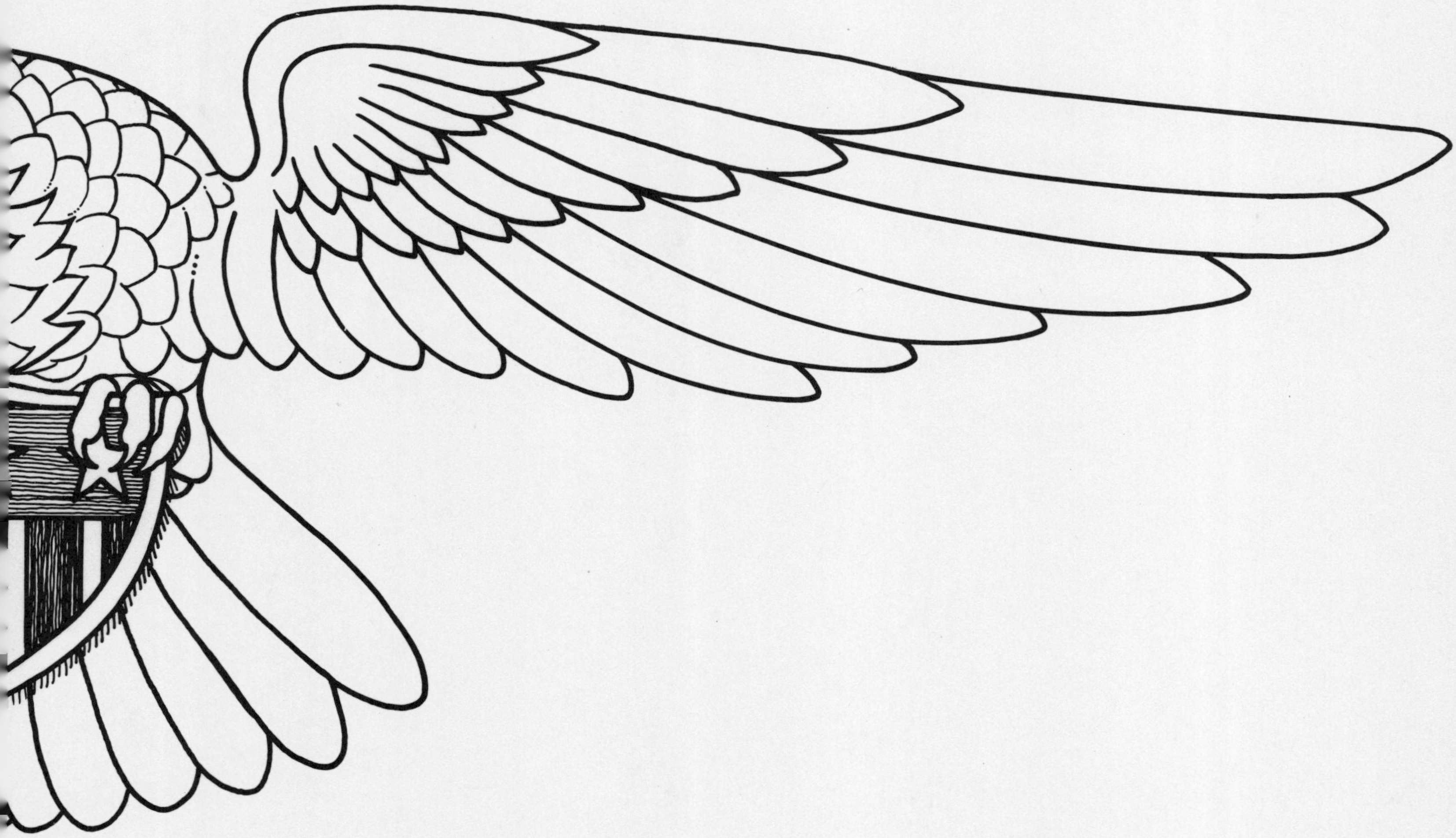

→

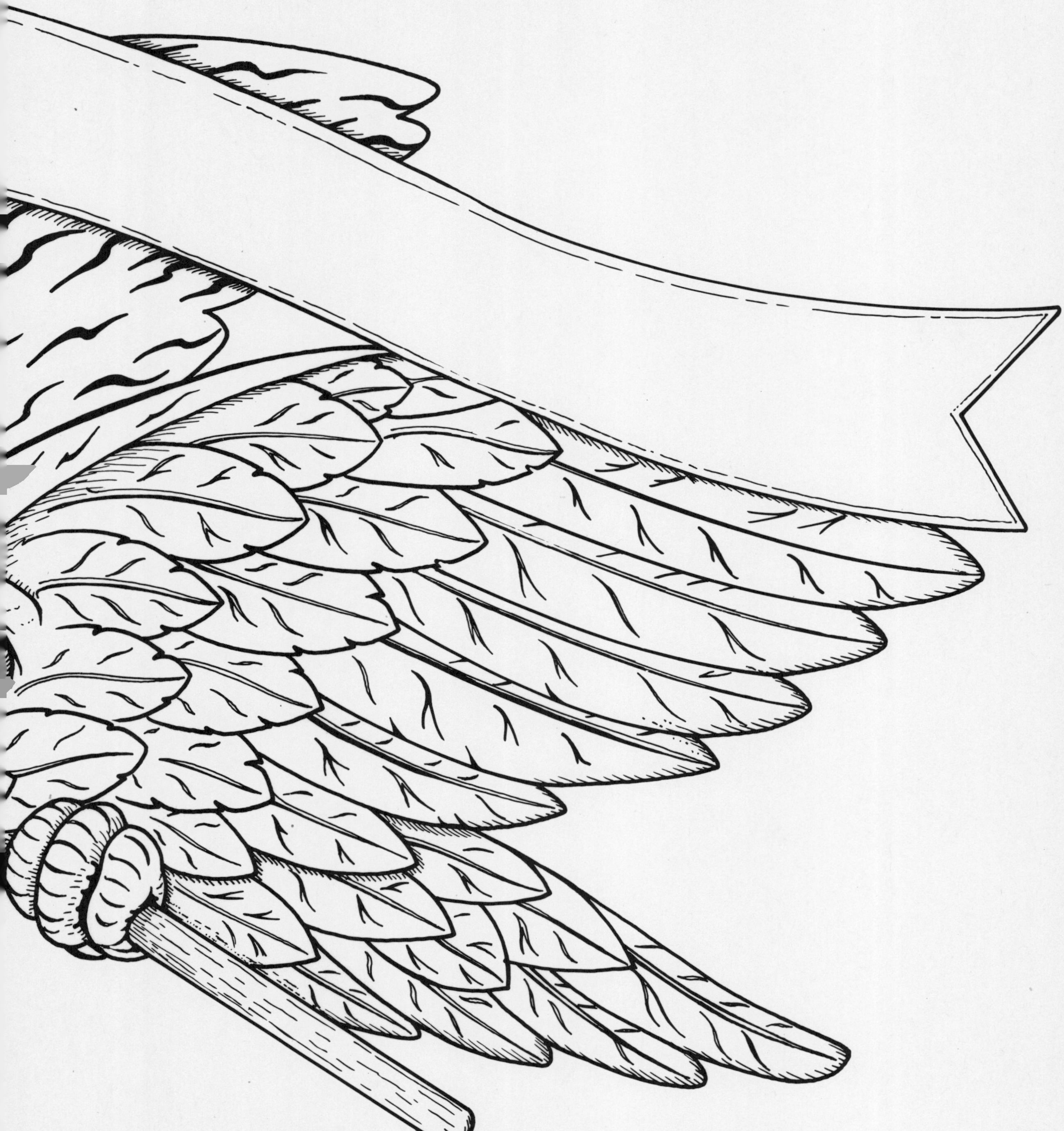

Remove staples to see and use full patterns. ***Plate 5 (right)***

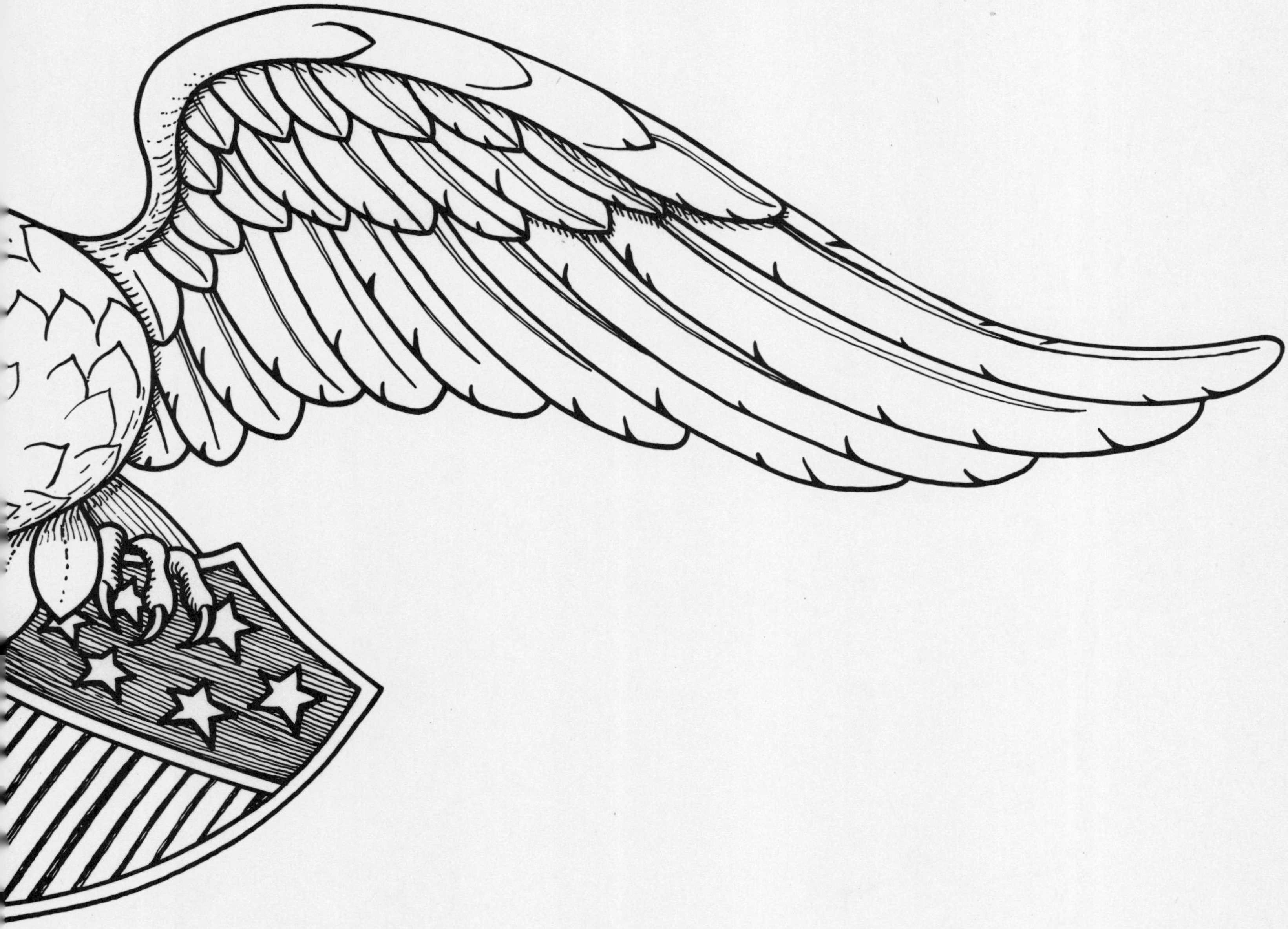

← Grain →

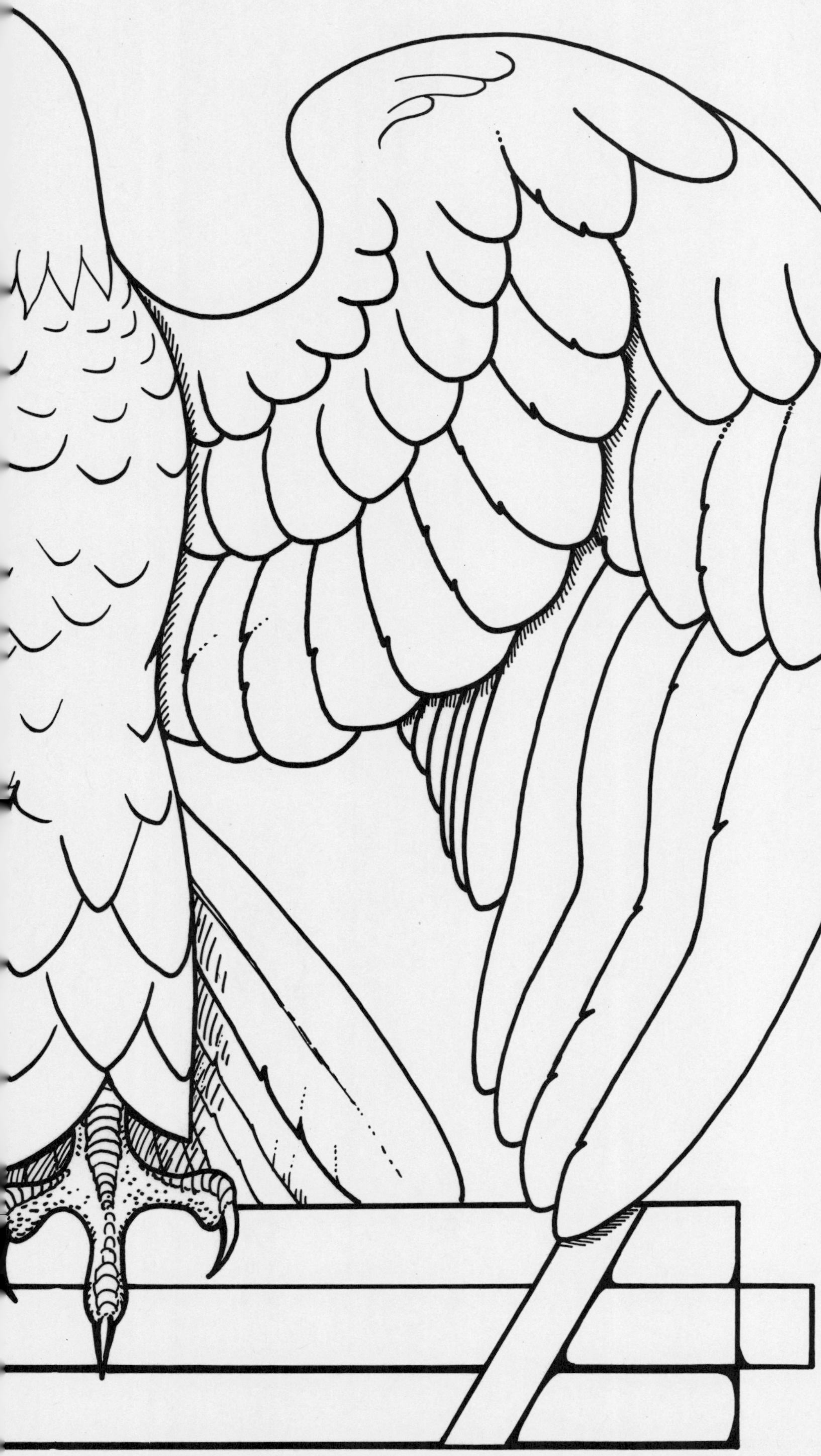

ı →

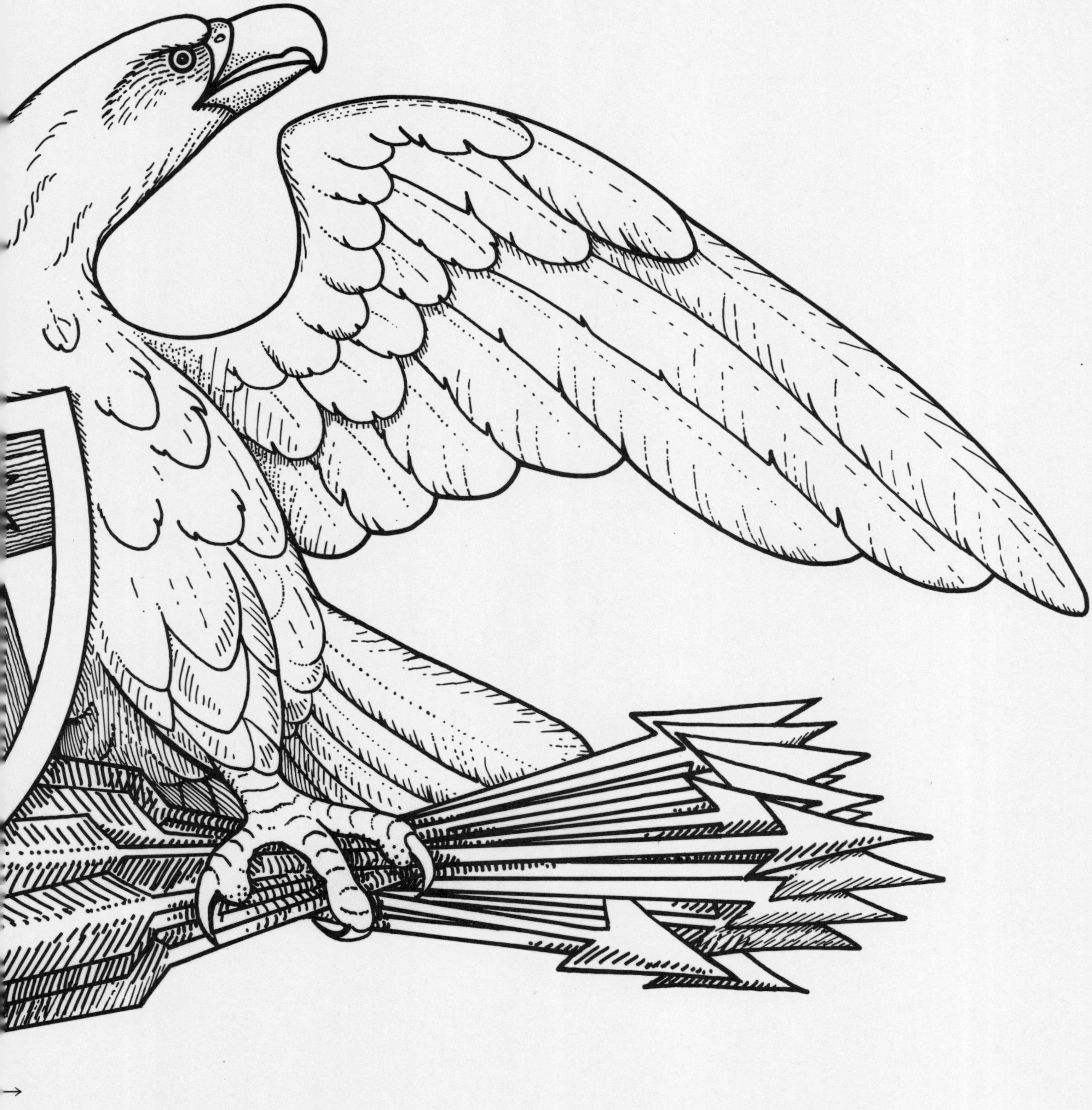

Remove staples to see and use full patterns. ***Plate 2 (right)***

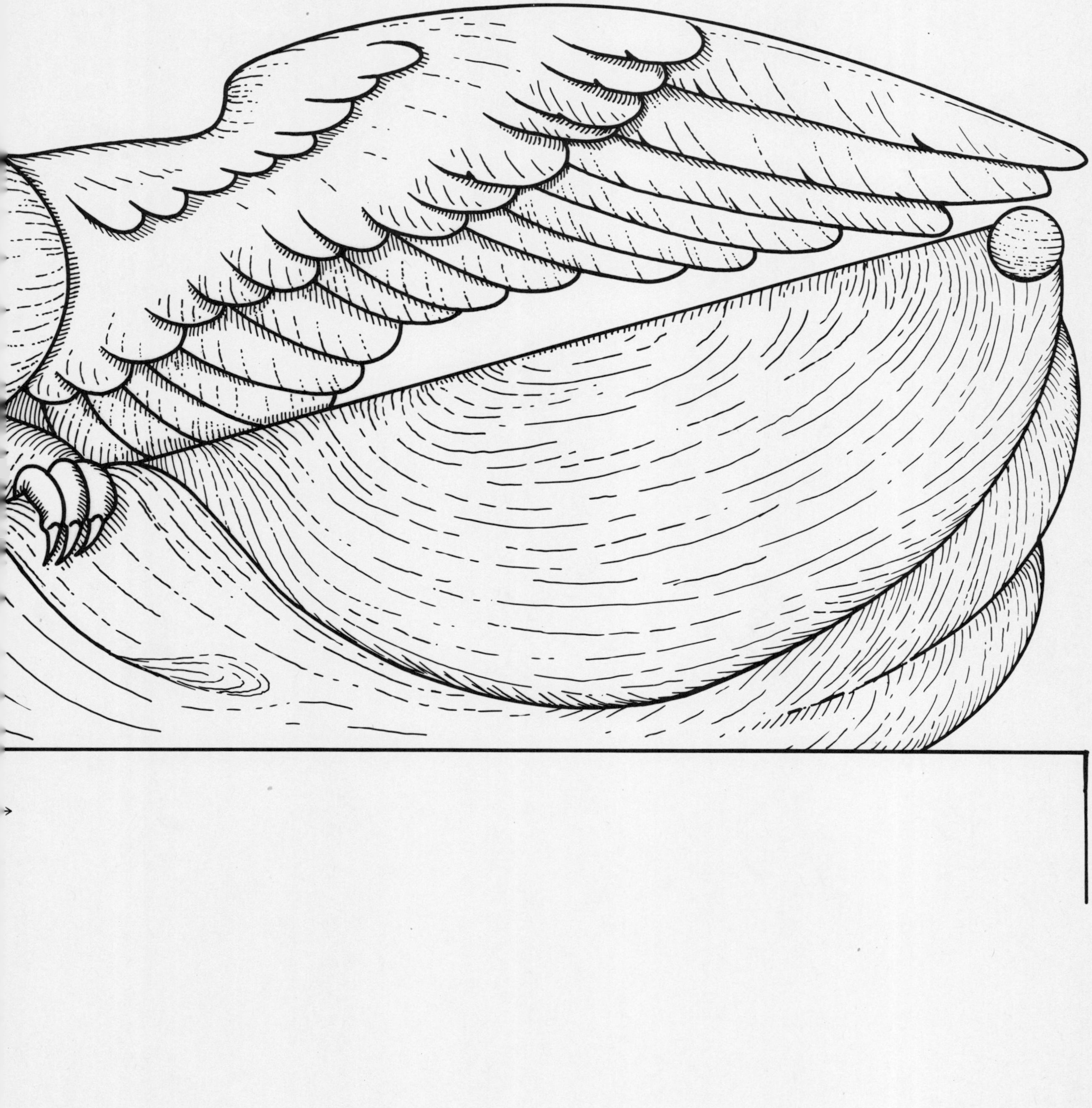

wood from the front of the wings. Thin and round the top and bottom edges, but be careful not to thin them too much. The thicker the wood, the stronger the plaque will be, and the easier to attach fastenings.

The next step—an essential one—is to cut around the outlines of the parts. (In relief carving, this is what is known as making *stop cuts.*) Using a sharp knife, cut straight down, at an angle of 90° to the surface. You should strive to cut not merely at right angles but also to a uniform *depth* around each feature. You may use a small, sharp chisel instead of a knife as long as you keep the edges of the outline smooth. Cut to a uniform depth of about ¼″.

Now work on the head. At this point the outline should look as in Fig. 3. Use a small #3 gouge to cut away wood around the *outside* of the head (not on the head itself), as in Fig. 4. After paring away any uneven gouge marks, sand this area smooth. Now you can round out the edges of the head itself and sand them smooth. Follow this procedure for the remaining areas in the foreground before you add any details such as the eye or feathers.

When you are ready to carve the details, refer

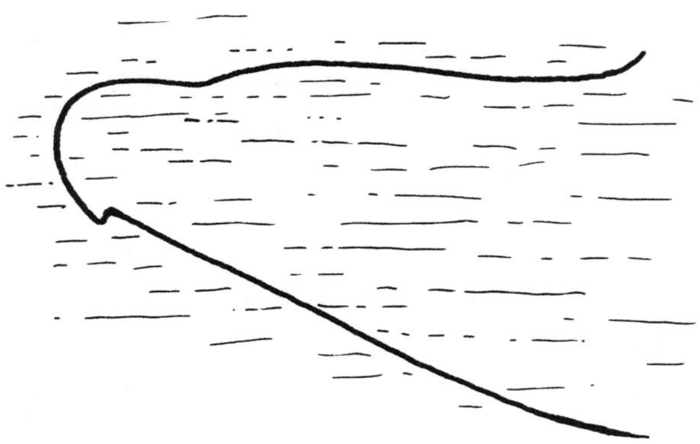

Fig. 3

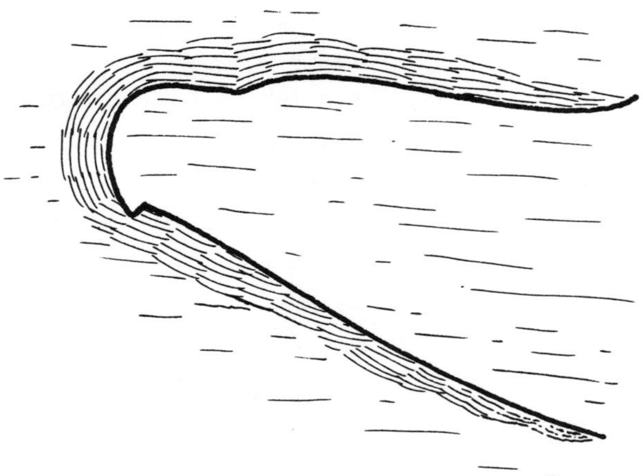

Fig. 4

to the patterns and lightly draw in these details with a pencil. Save the feathers for last; they will require particular attention, to be specified separately, below.

Fig. 5 shows the head with the eye, bill, and cere (fleshy area at the base of the bill, where an eagle's nostrils are) lightly outlined in pencil.

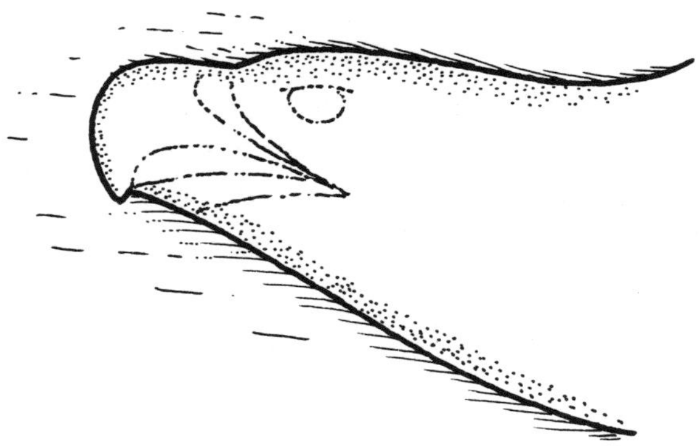

Fig. 5

Now you can use a knife to carve the details on the head. Cut firmly but not too deep. Always first cut the outline, at a 90° angle. You will then need to make "V" and similar relief cuts to achieve the proper effects, including opening the bill, separating toes, and delineating feathers. Fig. 6 shows an edge-on view of the completed head. Now carve the rest of the details, saving the wing feathers for last (except that you may wait until the very end to carve the contours of the flag).

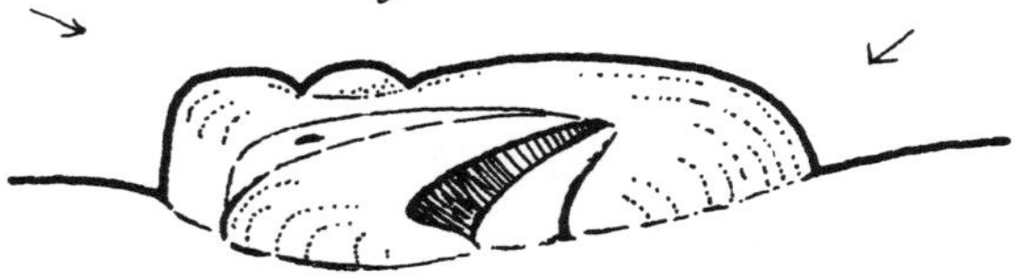

Fig. 6

Carving the wing feathers requires special attention. There are different ways to do this; the following procedure has worked well for me. First, in pencil, outline the feathers on the already contour-carved wings. When carving, always proceed from higher feathers to lower ones, and from the outside to the inside of the wing. Now, cut around the first feather with a sharp knife or chisel, cutting straight down as always, to form the outline. Smooth around the edges, using a small, shallow-sweep gouge to pare away wood. Do not cut away too much wood from the higher, outer feathers. When you proceed to the second and third feathers, and so on, continue as follows (I have found this method particularly effective). Taking feather number 2 as an example (see Fig. 7), cut the outline, then, using a small, shallow-sweep gouge, pare away wood just *outside* the margin on the side of feather 3. Smooth out the outline on that side. Then carve the surface of the feather, working *toward* feather number 1. To make the feathers seem to overlap, you may wish to cut slightly *under* feather 1. Then sand the outline of the feather to a smooth finish.

Using the above method, you will find that you have cut and sanded away the penciled outline. It is necessary to redraw this line as part of the outline of the next feather to be carved. This method of carving each feather in sequence and redrawing the outlines is time-consuming but will result in an attractive carving. The key to good feather delineation is the sequence of *draw, cut, gouge, and sand.* After all the feathers have been cut this way, you may, if required, cut in any slits or separated veins using a fine-bladed knife (see examples numbered 4 and 5 in Fig. 7).

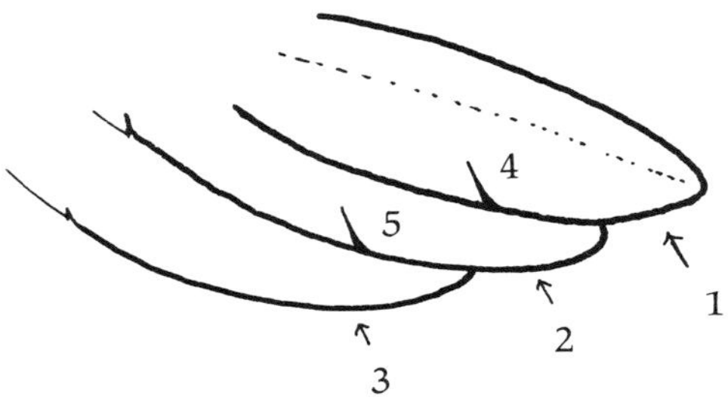

Fig. 7

A final word on this carving. The photograph on the cover shows the sternboard eagle resting on a base of unfinished wood. I actually carved both plaque and base from a single piece of wood, but, depending on the intended use of your carving, you may wish to carve just the eagle and flag and mount this piece either on a separate block of wood or on a wall or similar surface.

Carving Eagles in the Round

Carving the two free-standing eagles (Plates 8 through 10 and 12) requires the same techniques you would use to carve any figure "in the round." For carving the wing feathers, however, the techniques discussed above for relief carving may come in handy. The pilothouse eagle is so called from its use on the pilothouses of steamships in the late nineteenth century to indicate the presence of a local pilot.

On both the standing eagle (Plates 8, 9, and 10) and the pilothouse eagle (Plate 12), the wings and body are fully carved and sanded separately, and only then joined. On the standing eagle, I used glue and 1¼" siding nails to secure the wings. When you have attached the wings, and the glue has set, fill any gaps or seams with wood filler, let dry, and sand smooth.

Suggestions for Finishing

Many of the finest examples of early American Eagle carvings were gilded. The delicate covering of gold leaf beautifying and protecting these carvings was often truly magnificent. Obviously, it is impractical if not impossible for most of us today to finish our eagle carvings this way, although gold or other metallic paint, or a gilding wax, may be used to good effect. Depending on its intended location, a carving may be finished in a number of ways, or even left unfinished so it will quickly acquire a patina suggestive of a venerable antique.

The variety of stains, paints, varnishes, etc., available to the modern craftsperson is mind-boggling. Whichever you choose, remember to use an exterior finish on a carving that will be exposed to the weather. I use exterior finishes almost exclusively. Another point to remember is that if you intend to use latex or acrylic paint on your carving, begin with latex or acrylic primer only. You may instead cover the latex or acrylic primer with oil paint, but *never cover oil primer with anything but oil paint.* The cover photographs of the carvings offer finishing suggestions that you may alter to suit your taste.

Some final reminders: Follow all the special instructions, indications of scale, etc., given on the plates with the patterns. Always take into consideration the direction of the grain in the wood. And remember that certain patterns are for reference only and cannot be used as templates. Have fun making your decorative eagle carvings!